Managing Anxiety

Managing Anxiety

Peter Koestenbaum

Celestial Arts
Millbrae, California

We are grateful to the following publishers for their permission to quote from the works listed below.

To Little, Brown and Company and George Allen and Unwin Ltd., for permission to reprint the Frontispiece "To Edith," from *The Autobiography of Bertrand Russell.* Copyright 1951, 1952, 1953, 1956 by Bertrand Russell. Copyright © by Allen and Unwin Ltd. Copyright © 1967 by George Allen and Unwin Ltd.

To Seabury Press and Ediciones Carlos Lohlé, for permission to reprint a selection from Ernesto Cardenal's *To Live Is to Love,* translated by Kurt Reinhardt. Ediciones Carlos Lohlé is the publisher of the original Spanish-language version, *Vida en el Amor.*

Note: The names, places and identifying circumstances of the illustrative materials in this book have been changed to protect the anonymity of my students. Diana is not a real person, but a collage, as is her letter, derived from those of several women.

Celestial Arts
231 Adrian Road
Millbrae, California 94030

First Printing, July 1979

Made in the United States of America

Library of Congress Cataloging in Publication Data

Koestenbaum, Peter, 1928–
 Managing anxiety.

 Includes bibiliographical references and index.
 1. Anxiety.   2. Consciousness.   3. Title
BF575.A6K6 1979   616.8'52   74-8555
ISBN 0-89087-248-1

1 2 3 4 5 6 7 / 85 84 83 82 80 81 79

Contents

This book is dedicated to
my private students in philosophy

*Behold a good doctrine
has been given you;
forsake it not*

Proverbs 4:2

Introduction

Philosophy is the most ancient of the healing arts. It has traditionally been assigned the task of helping us with the anxieties
that are the inevitable accompaniments of life. An important
branch of philosophy today—sometimes called *phenomenology* or *existentialism,* but also having its roots in the many
varieties of Eastern thought—seeks to fulfill that ancient
philosophic duty. This popular and relevant form of philosophy studies the nature of human consciousness—a necessary
step if one is to apply philosophy to human problems.

The human problem area that concerns us here is anxiety.
Anxiety has many forms and it afflicts all of us; I use the word
pain, or sometimes *suffering,* to designate all the negative
aspects of life—that is, those aspects usually thought to be un-
desirable. When we have examined that mysterious entity
known as consciousness or awareness, then we can explore constructive ways to handle the pain of anxiety.

Always remember: Philosophy is the central business of life.
Everything follows from your philosophical world view. Therapy and medicine, money and success, and all similar values
derive from your basic philosophy of humankind. Existential
philosophy represents our pursuit of the authentic meaning of
human fulfillment. Every one of us needs a philosophy of life.
The more competent and thoughtful we are, the more accurate is our philosophy of life, and the more successful will it be
to sustain, protect, and guide us.

The theme of this book—the compassionate understanding

of human beings—could well be summed up in the following
passage from Bertrand Russell's autobiography:

Love and knowledge, so far as they were possible, led upward toward
the heavens. But always pity brought me back to earth. Echoes of
cries of pain reverberate in my heart. Children in famine, victims
tortured by oppressors, helpless old people a hated burden to their
sons, and the whole world of loneliness, poverty, and pain make a
mockery of what human life should be. I long to alleviate the evil,
but I cannot, and I too suffer.*

Pity is not enough. Philosophy must demonstrate that it has an
aggressive program for the conquest of suffering—both for individuals and for society.

A home is a part of the universe that belongs permanently to
one individual person. You need a home, an eternally protec-
tive slice of the cosmos, as your very own. You need to be an-
chored, so that no power on earth nor in the heavens above
can ever dislodge you. A true home should protect you against
such dangers as attack, injustice, and theft, and also against
poverty, hunger, anxiety, disease, old age, and even death. An
authentic home is like a warm mother: It soothes your pain,
wipes your tears, quenches your thirst, and feeds your hunger.
A genuine home is like God creating Adam, because a true
home defines you: It tells you who you are; it gives you an
identity. It makes you unique; it gives you individuality.
Philosophy can help the homeless find a home.

For example, at one time you may have asked yourself, "Am
I to be sensitive, artistic, delicate, and endowed with deep feelings? Or am I to be a rough, tough, single-minded pioneering
type?" A true home will answer that question for you, because
it determines your values and describes your roles in life. You
undoubtedly have asked yourself "Am I treating my parents
(or my children, my spouse, or myself) as I should? Is my conscience clear, or do I feel guilt about the way I behave toward

---

*The Autobiography of Bertrand Russell (Boston: Little, Brown and Co.,
1967), p. 4.

them?" What is right? To declare your independence and tell your mother to leave you alone, or to invite her to live with you, or even to move in with her? Your true home answers that question for you with absolute certainty and authority; it informs you what you must do to resolve your guilts. A true home will tell you precisely, in every specific situation, what your duty is to your parents, yourself, your children, and how the conflicts that arise should be resolved. A true home informs you of your precise duties to your country, to God, and to each one of your fellow men and women.

A true home gives you correct answers about what is the right personality for you. "Should I drift or should I achieve?" "Should I conform or be independent?" "Should I live for the now or for the future? For pleasure or for duty?" A home responds to these questions and thus relieves you of anxiety and guilt. What makes a home your home is your knowledge that the answers are true. A home is also where you find the bliss of forgiveness. A home will always take you back and always love you, if you return, surrender, and confess your trespasses.

Now ask yourself with naked honesty and innocent candor, "Do *I* have answers to life's important questions?" Does it hurt me not to have answers?" "Does it pain me if whatever answers I do have are neither certain nor accurate?" If you have answers, you have a home. Since you are reading this book, chances are you probably do not have reliable answers in final matters concerning life and death. And if you do not have answers, then you do not have a home, though you know at the same time that such a home is an absolute necessity.

Philosophy is the search for that home — a search without illusions. Today existential philosophy makes us aware that this home is no longer found where our ancestors looked for it — the farm, the family, the church, the country, the flag, the party, the cause. Traditional avenues of finding a home have failed dismally and continue to fail. And attempts to maintain a stiff upper lip — the aggressive facade of the pseudo-adult — produce symptoms but not security, create anesthesia but not authenticity.

Modern civilization has made people homeless. Perhaps it is more accurate to say that humans have always been homeless, but the technological explosion of this century has forced most of us to become painfully aware of the real meaning of that relentless homelessness. We might say that people of previous ages were blessed with blindness about this lack. Today parents divorce depriving their children of the family into which they were born, and children thus receive their first lesson in homelessness. Similarly, society dictates that children eventually leave their parents' home to make a life for themselves. As a consequence, neither parents nor children are the same when (and if) they do meet again. They become strangers, often losing forever the connection that meant home to them. Thus, as children grow up, they get free instruction in alienation. Nor does closeness to the land offer any succor. Many people have traveled back to the land of their ancestors hoping to recapture their true homes. They have always been disappointed, because being uprooted from the soil is a lesson in starvation.

Jerry, a black student whose family came from Alabama, thought he could find his true home by taking a trip to Ghana, with the possibility of settling there permanently. Although he felt he was a stranger in the U.S., he believed he would achieve a profound feeling of homecoming when he arrived in Africa. Unfortunately it did not work out that way for Jerry. He was even more of a stranger in Accra than in San Francisco. It took him a long and expensive trip to make the philosophical discovery of all contemporary individuals: that humans, though desperately in need of a home, do not have one merely by virtue of being born into a family, a race, a nation.

Ruben has a similar story to tell. His family emigrated from Poland to America during the Nazi persecution of Jews in World War II. His yearning for his ancestral home is seen in the fact that he has never lost his Polish accent nor his fluency in Yiddish. He finally managed to make his pilgrimage to Jerusalem. Arriving at the Wailing Wall at last, where he thought he was going to find his true home, he wept; but he wept not with joy because he was home, but with the darkest anguish because he now knew that his home was nowhere in the tangible world. After the Wailing Wall, no other place was left to look for home. It cost him a heartbreaking experience to discover in his own life—in his flesh, blood, and bones—the philosophic truth that human beings are homeless. This tragic knowledge may mean little when expounded theoretically in a philosophy book; but it means a great deal if experienced as ultimate disappointment and dark emptiness at the Wailing Wall in Jerusalem.

Paul, recently divorced, went back to the Kansas farm of his parents, having lived in Vancouver, Canada, most of his life. But rather than finding his true home, he found there a couple of strangers in a land he had never really known.

John and Cindy took to the wilderness. They went homesteading in Alaska in search of humanity's authentic ancestral home. They lived romantically and wrote like Thoreau. But did they find a true home? Their bodies relaxed and their health improved, but it was only the envy of those they left behind that supported their wavering conviction that indeed they had found their home. John and Cindy ultimately discovered that, far from finding a home, they had brought their homelessness with them all the way north to Alaska. Their original question was, could the problem of homelessness—which resisted all solutions in Boston—be solved in Alaska instead? Their answer was *no*.

History and culture are filled with ersatz homes, with phony roots, and with surrogate foundations. There are myths and rituals, prejudices and cliches which try to lull us into believing there does exist a home for us. A very religious person may feel that rigorous and mechanical adherence to dietary laws, liturgy, prayers, rituals, and church attendance will provide his home. But many an educated, modern person can no longer be adequately satisfied with such a mechanical approach; neither intellect nor emotions permit the exchange of compulsive behavior for an authentic home. A contemporary enlightened individual rightfully doubts that a home can really be found in ritual and dogma. The rugged American male, complete with trailer, boat, and gun may hope that reminiscing about his pioneer past and mimicking the life of an early American while at the same time perceiving himself from the vantage point of a late twentieth-century American suburbanite, will provide a home for him. Instead he is apt to get mosquito bites and debts; he is as homeless as before. The most he can hope for, if indeed his camping has esthetic content for him, is that in the solitude of the High Sierras or in the misty expanse of the Pacific Ocean (which Alan Watts called the edge of the world) he will confront and touch that abysmal aloneness, that singular point which is the deliciously purified and agonizingly ecstatic recognition of his essential homelessness. Perhaps with these almost unbearable realizations he can begin to find his true home through the philosophic pursuit of the nature of his being.

Much advertising promises to take you home, to give you a home, if only you buy a certain brand of cigarettes, whiskey, deodorant, or clothing. Such advertising is fraudulent and cynical, because it does not inform or deliver but instead preys on a real need. Even the actual purchase of a home is confused with this basic human need. Too many people believe that the transactions in a real estate office are in some way connected to their fundamental need for a true home. Before the purchase such a person may have been a *wandering* searcher for a home only to become a mortgage-bound *stationary* searcher for a home. Too many people are ensnared and enslaved by real estate — under the illusion that they fell in love with the view, the neighborhood, the floor plan, the kitchen, or the tax advantages — into believing that the human problem of homelessness can be managed through a thirty- or forty-year-long indebtedness. If anything at all is achieved, it is that the *distraction* from the real problem is now made permanent. What a pity, especially if we consider that this is the only life we are likely to have!

Philosophy, especially as the existential way of life, can deal with the problem of our home. The basic message of responsi-

ble existential philosophy in answer to the problem of alienation is this: *the dependable and imperishable home exists in
the individual, subjective, and inward spirit of every human
being.* By the generic expression *existential philosophy* I mean
all of those contemporary philosophical views that study the
structure and the health of that miraculous and mysterious
phenomenon which we call human consciousness.

Home is the consciousness that each of us *is* in our silent and
solitary centers. It is the consciousness that is aroused when
two individuals meet in love, not in sex. Home is the consciousness that is in touch with the cosmic stream, that senses
its oneness with the life of the universe itself. To understand
and to experience that individual conscious center is to have
found our home. That insight can be integrated into all aspects of life. A home can be found and it can be shared. The
path home is through philosophy, through insight and intro-
spection into consciousness. We cannot come home through
the expenditure of vast sums of money or expensive moves, or
through divorces or gadgets, but only through the discovery of
our sacred inward nature.

It is not necessary to be a professional philosopher to understand these issues and their attempted answers. Familiarity
with the philosophical foundations of these insights is no guarantee that one will discover a true home and live there, any
more than the study of medicine produces health or the study
of economics produces wealth. Each of us needs to build on
our own a workable philosophy of life.

People with problems, and that means all of us, today turn
for help to psychiatry, psychology, medicine, and pharmacology. Philosophy, however, is the oldest of all the healing arts.
The accumulated wisdom of philosophy, especially the existential philosophy that has developed in recent decades, can
serve as a basis for resolving many of our daily problems—such
as success, love, and raising children, as well as such problems
as anxiety, guilt, and depression. Moreover, not all problems
are signs of illness. There are stresses and other problems that

are symptoms of health. It is the task of philosophy to help us, not with our disease, but with our condition of health. The inevitable fact of anxiety is a case in point. Medicine can alleviate anxiety; philosophy can give meaning to anxiety. Drugs can allay suffering, but they cannot produce either meaning or love.

The everyday use of philosophy for the purpose of enhancing one's life and solving its deepest problems is as old as Socrates and ancient Tibet, but also as new as space exploration. The general benefits of medicine, psychiatry, psychology, and pharmacology have been widely publicized and have been made generally available. Philosophy, infinitely older than these sciences, has mostly been the property of those introduced to its scholarly technicalities and conceptual intricacies. The general public senses, accurately, a great philosophic vacuum and demands, justifiably, that this emptiness be filled. Today a vast communication gap exists between the insights of a "professional on human nature" and the so-called general public. This gap is both unhealthy and unfair. Other sciences have bridged this gap; it is now necessary for philosophy to do the same.

You know that medicine and chemistry as well as psychology and engineering can help to make a better life for you. But what can philosophy do for you? Do you know that the real issues, the deepest issues in your life—the issues that precede all others—can only be handled with philosophy, not with engineering, physics, or psychiatry? Medicine cannot save you from death—it can only postpone the end. Philosophy can help you deal successfully with that inevitable limit to your life. Psychiatry can cure a phobia but it cannot deal with the philosophical problem of how to manage your free will and the anxiety and responsibility that accompany it. Psychiatry cannot eliminate the anguish that comes from freedom in making choices—it can only ameliorate the pathological expressions of that anguish. Philosophy can show you how anguish teaches you about yourself and others. In fact, you need philosophy far more than technology in order to live well. That point is forgotten in the desperate speed and chaos of the modern world.

In life there are two kinds of emergency: sickness and health. In our society we tend to recognize only the first of these as real. Sickness means pain, often unbearable pain. Here is our first emergency. We then run to a healer for help. We believe that once the pain is stilled we are truly healed.

However, what is usually called health is but a beginning, never an end. When we are in good physical and mental health we have not concluded our life's destiny. On the contrary, we have merely equipped ourselves to move on to the second emergency: how to live well, how to fulfill our destiny, and how to give our life true meaning.

John B. has devoted the first half-century of his life to developing a successful restaurant chain. He has devoted all of his physical and psychological powers to business success. That was his response to the first emergency—his specific and individual pain was his lack of financial security. His goal—a substantial and secure income—has now been attained. Having reached this destination, John B. discovers that meeting his first emergency leads to his second emergency, expressed in the question "What is the meaning of life?" In a way, John B. is now ready for his second career, in the sense in which all people, upon entering the second half of their lives, are ready for philosophy. But what is that career to be? He has prepared himself for *something,* it seems, during his first fifty years. But what is that evasive something for which all this extraordinary preparation is intended? Many, having concluded this period of preparation in life and having achieved what appears to outsiders as the culmination of their careers, now face their *second* emergency—and become lost. John's second emergency is the question of what will give significance to his life. How should he use his newly acquired freedom? How can he meet his eventual death? How can he conquer, or accommodate himself to, the inexorable movement of time? Of what value are his accomplishments when all values are called in question and when all life ends in death anyway?

While our lives differ markedly one from the other, all of us must come to grips with the two emergencies of life sooner or later. Reflect on the following questions and give serious answers to them, preferably in writing. In this way, you may begin a journal to accompany your readings and reflections in the existential way of life.

Do you think that the second emergency is deeper than the first? Do you think you should answer the second emergency—the problem of meaning in life—before you handle the first—financial solvency? Do you think that failure to deal with the first emergency is but an escape from facing the second and much more serious emergency? As long as you must watch calories to control your weight, swallow pills to control your blood pressure, work sixteen hours a day to establish financial freedom, as long as all these efforts are needed to meet your first emergency, there can be no time to handle the second. Do you experience that as a relief? The first emergency has answers— You can consult the experts: doctors, therapists, economists, educators, etc. But does the second emergency have answers? The second emergency is deeper and more important than the first. "Success" in life may really be an escape from philosophy. What do *you* think?

PART 1

Consciousness

1

Metaphors for Consciousness

Our consciousness shapes our ego and our world. A general idea of the nature of human consciousness will prepare us to consider how such a view can be applied to the problems of living. The specific features of consciousness include the following: (1) Consciousness is continuous with, but different from, its objects in the world. These objects range from such presumably *subjective* objects as feelings, ideas, and concepts to objects usually acknowledged as such, including human bodies, trees, and planets. (2) The relation between subject and object, consciousness and the world—or, in the language of traditional philosophy, the mind-body connection—can be thought of as a *field.* On the one end (subjective end) the field is transparent, like a void. On the other end, the field is solid and concrete. There is no specific border in which mind becomes matter. The area of connection is more like a gradually thickening fog. The region symbolized by the void is called consciousness or subjectivity, whereas the region symbolized by concreteness is called world or objectivity. (3) I believe that we know the truth of the field theory of consciousness through direct and unprejudiced inspection of the general nature of our human experience. Finally, (4) the consequences of this view are both dramatic and health-producing.

At this point it is helpful to clarify the meaning of consciousness by introducing some metaphors.

1. *A person is a river.* The life of each individual is like a river; it flows into the space beyond and into the time of the future. It is more accurate and therefore better to say that people are rivers that flow than to say they are bodies that are

3

static. Human beings are more like space capsules hurtling into the future than groupings of molecules forming societies of cells. Humanity's sense of flowing union with nature and with the universe is a more accurate description than the belief that humans exist separated from the world around them.

2. *The field-of-consciousness theory.* The life of each individual is an amorphous *field,* a process, and a continuum, rather than a thing with clear limits or an object with sharp boundaries. Specifically, a human being is like a magnetic field, where the positive and negative poles are, respectively, person as subject and person as object, person as consciousness and person as the world, person as mind and person as body, and person as awareness and person as behavior.

Important consequences follow from this analogy. For one, the mind is not *in* the body, just as the magnet's positive pole is not *in* its negative pole. The mind is outside the body in the same sense that the positive pole is outside the negative pole. Finally, to continue with our metaphor, the existence of the body is dependent on and brought about by the existence of the mind in the same way that the existence of the negative pole of the magnet is dependent on and brought about by the existence of the positive pole. A positive pole—as is the case with a positive electrical charge—automatically and instantaneously creates an equal and opposing charge beyond and outside itself.

The metaphor of the magnet must be taken seriously. The idea of a field, used prevalently in physics, is made possible by the fact that a human being's existence in this world is a continuous and bipolar field rather than a collection of isolated objects or things. I do not think the converse is true—namely, that the field theory of consciousness is grafted onto an image borrowed from physics or from farming (as in "a wheat field"). The field of consciousness theory of humankind radically transforms our ideas about the relation between mind and body.

3. *Human beings and their world.* A fish is nothing without its ecosystem and a human being is nothing without his or her

world. But the fish is not sea or aquarium and a person is not world or body. Human being and world, consciousness and objects, like fish and aquarium, are interdependent, but without either of them losing identity, individuality, uniqueness, independence, and difference.

4. *The comet theory.* Closely following the field-of-consciousness theory is the idea that all things exist only, and always, in a field of perception. And perception is a manifestation of consciousness. We call this the *comet theory of objects.* Each object—whether it be a tree or a cloud, an idea or a feeling, my body or my behavior (all of which are objects to my consciousness)—is like a flaming comet, attached to which is a long and luminous tail. Similarly, every object is not merely a thing that exists by itself but also has attached to it a "tail" or a stream of consciousness. A tree is not simply a tree, but it is a tree-seen-by-an-observer. And my experience, of course, discloses that this observer is always "I." A mathematical concept is not the bare concept but a concept-thought-by-a-person. If I think of a person perceiving a tree, then the tree is really a tree-observed-by-a-person-observed-by-me. Moreover, I-observe-an-observer-observing-a-mathematical-concept; that is the total nature of a concept. Everything you perceive in the universe has a string attached to it that connects directly to you. The tether is always there, although sometimes it is tenuous and can be experientially detected only through meditation, a stepping back *into* consciousness and *out of* involvement with life.

The comet theory of objects has been successfully applied to a kind of psychotherapy called existential family counseling. A San Diego therapist uses a large plastic cube with transparent windows on each of its six sides, which serves to illustrate the point that every object or event (such as a family situation) has many subjective sides to it. And unless we get a *complete* picture we do not get any picture at all. The cube suggests that so-called objective solutions to family problems represent an unreal quest. The individual subjective perceptions must be included in any family argument before we have a true picture of the situation. Each of the six transparent windows of the cube is of a different color. In the center of the cube is affixed a small globe. That globe represents the family, which is seen in several different ways through the variously colored windows. As you look through any of the individually colored transparent plastic windows you can see the globe as well as the remaining five windows. Shifting from one transparent window to another, you notice that the globe changes color with the changing color of each new window and that the colors of the other visible windows also change. In other words, each window provides a particular, individualized, and different coloration of the world and of each of the other windows to that world.

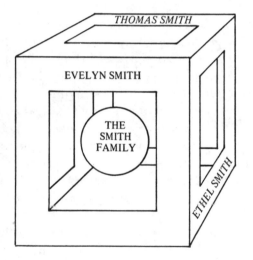

When the Smith family visited the therapist he used the cube in the following way. Mrs. Smith initially came for counseling because her second daughter, thirteen-year-old Evelyn, had become more and more intractable at home. "The entire family is in a constant uproar because of Evelyn," she said. The therapist suggested that all four family members come in for counseling. The whole family, not Evelyn alone, had a problem.

The first step in therapy was to ask each family member to develop his or her own diagnosis of the total family situation. "What is the matter with the family?" the therapist asked each member in turn. Everyone, of course, had a different opinion. Thomas, the father, felt that his wife did not spend enough time with Evelyn. "Ethel is never home when Evelyn returns from school, and she expects me, after a hard day at the plant, to take care of the problem," he complained. Teresa, Evelyn's fifteen-year-old sister, felt that Evelyn needed more discipline than she had been getting because, as Teresa put it, "Evelyn always interferes with everything I do. She listens in on my phone calls, she turns the TV on high when I do homework, she wakes me up early in the mornings on weekends." And Evelyn herself could only cry and mutter "No one understands me" when she was asked to diagnose the family's needs.

The therapist then took a crayon and wrote a different family member's name over each of the windows of the cube. Over the fifth window he wrote his own name and over the sixth he simply wrote "Grandma." "Let's find out what troubles this family," he started. "What does this family truly look like?"

"The family, you think, is the small globe inside. The globe looks different to each one of you. Look!" And he asked each member to view the family (small globe) and its other members (windows) and then to describe to the others what was seen. Obviously, everyone saw something different. He then added, "It also looks different to Grandma and different to me."

The lesson the therapist was teaching is that no objective family reality exists; there is in this world no object that can be called "the Smith family." There exists only a series of subject-object fields, relations, and connections. The *problem*—experienced as emotional pain—is the mistaken belief that the family is a thing. The solution—experienced as relief, resolution, and joy—is the knowledge that the family is a series of subject-object fields, each of which is partially the same as the others and partially different from them.

A family is a conglomerate of subjective ways of perceiving

the common object "family" (the small globe) *and* the un-
common subjectivities of the other family members (the other
windows). We must remember that each object has a conscious or subjective tail or string attached to it. Even though
there is only *one* globe (one family), there are six window-
globe combinations. The true family is not the uniform central globe but the sum of the six window-globe combinations.

In this way the therapist introduces a decent respect for the
legitimacy of each one of the family's personal centers and for
the reality of each individual perspective. Such a new way of
perceiving a family structure, within the context of a field-of-
consciousness theory of humankind, creates a healthy respect
for one's own needs and an ethical toleration for the needs of
others.

The therapist can now point out to Mrs. Smith that what
appears to her as a serious problem does not seem that way at
all to him. Mrs. Smith's window colors the family "troubled,"
whereas the therapist's window colors it "normal." Thomas'
window colors the family as "burdensome," whereas Evelyn's
window colors the family as "unfair." Furthermore, Mrs.
Smith's window colors Evelyn's window as "guilty and irresponsible," while Evelyn's window colors Mrs. Smith's window
as "insensitive" and even as "hateful." After this analysis, the
family atmosphere changed from one of domination and control to one of letting be, from rigidity to freedom.

5. *Consciousness and body.* The mind-body and person-
world boundaries are like a beach. The beach is an ambiguous
and interpenetrating, oscillating boundary between land and
sea. Land and sea are precisely defined and conspicuously different from each other. Yet their boundary is always unclear
and always changing—quickly with the waves and slowly with
the tides. The same is true of the mind-body, consciousness-
world, and person-environment separation. As the sea is unlike the land, so consciousness is unlike the body; but as sea
and land together make a single beach, so consciousness and
body unify to make a single person.

6. *A human being is a sunburst.* We move now from what

has been a series of linear metaphors to circular and spherical ones. A human being is a field like a sunburst, like the solar system. A person's silent consciousness is the super-heated center of the sun. Actions and perceptions, feelings and aspirations, thoughts and hopes, language, breath, and vision are the rays radiating into vastness of space. And, finally, the individual's body, behavior, society, beliefs, people, and world are the objects that are illuminated by this light.

If the solar system could think and if it were as philosophically ignorant as human beings, it would believe that it is only comprised of the planets. It would think its total nature is the planets alone. It would be completely unaware of the sun and its rays that make the illumination of the planets possible in the first place.

The sunburst is the complete solar system — sun, rays, and planets — and not just the planets on its periphery. And the total person is not body or world, but the sunburst, the total consciousness-body-world field.

7. *Humankind and explosion.* A human being is a field like an explosion. A person is first of all the center which is empty, evacuated, hollow; second, the flying shrapnel, the onrushing air, and the expanding shockwaves; third, and finally, the target, the crater in the ground, or the collapsed structure. The total explosion is the total field from center to target. Similarly, the total person is the total field from inner consciousness to external body, society, and world.

8. *A human being is time.* The experience of the forward movement of time is identical with the experience of the growth and futurization of our consciousness. Human consciousness and the experience of time are synonymous. They can serve to clarify and illustrate each other.

As time moves, so does consciousness; both emerge from a past, through a present, into the future. One is called the passage of time and the other is called growth, transcendence, process, and fulfillment.

Time does not occur, exist, or flow *in* something, like a matrix, or *on* something, like a base. It may be true that time is a river, but the metaphor is forced. A river has a bed on which it flows. Time has no such bed. Time is ultimate and irreducible. Time cannot be perceived from a perspective that is outside of time. Unlike the river, there can be for time no movement or emergence prior to time or more basic than time or in which time takes place. Time cannot be explained in terms of more primitive concepts; in fact, life is time, the universe is time.

Lived time, experienced time — unlike its meaning in modern physics — is not produced by measurement. On the contrary, measurement makes sense only because *to be* means to be temporal, *to be* means to be time. Measurement is a phenomenon that occurs *in* time. What applies to time is also true of the field that is our individual consciousness. Consciousness does not exist *in* something else nor as a product *of* something else. Like time, consciousness is irreducible and primary. Consciousness is certainly not the product of chemical and molecular interactions. On the contrary, these latter can be understood only in and by consciousness. Nor is consciousness the result of a long chain of biological and anthropological evolution. Evolution is a theory constructed by and sustained in consciousness. Consciousness, like time, has always been and always will be. There is no "other" consciousness in which "this" consciousness exists, just as there is no "superior" time or "meta"-time in which "regular" time exists. There is only time and there is only consciousness, and these are one ultimate.

Time does not have an underlying matrix because it already is the last matrix. It is similar to consciousness; consciousness does not rest on something prior, because it is already the *most* prior aspect of all existence. And temporal consciousness is the field-of-consciousness flow whose running, movement, and energy I experience as *my unique life.*

The psychological equivalent of knowing that I am time is successful living, because success in life means unceasing progress in the process of psychological growth.

The ghost-in-a-machine theory. Borrowing a phrase from Gilbert Ryle, the ghost-in-a-machine theory views human beings as organisms or machines—and nothing else. They operate by the laws of chemistry and mechanics. Their minds, consciousnesses, or souls are not real. They are ghosts hiding somewhere within the wheels and springs and transistors of those machines, or lodged between the organs of those bodies. According to this view, the mind is the result of chemical events and developments in the brain; culture and human values are the result of thousands of years of anthropological, apelike behavioral development. There is no understanding whatever that a human being is a consciousness, a subjectivity, a unique ego, an inwardness, and even a soul. In my opinion, this theory is *false* in that it contradicts the simplest and most obvious facts of human experience. Furthermore, it is *dangerous* because it dehumanizes people by destroying the most precious achievement of culture—namely, the history of consciousness.

What are the consequences of the ghost-in-a-machine theory? Today, this materialistic self-concept is integrated into most of our private and public affairs. Unfortunately, that theory leads to symptom formation. We know how the ghost-in-a-machine theory of man has been tacitly adopted by the society in which we live. It is taught in the schools and it is presupposed in medicine, psychology, and psychiatry. It underlies our political decisions and describes the patterns in which the nation spends its money.

There are, I believe, eight specific consequences that follow from living the ghost-in-a-machine theory rather than the field-of-consciousness theory.

1. The "ghost" theory expresses itself as *inconsiderateness* in relations among people. It leads to lack of respect for human beings, including oneself. The individual who lives by this theory cannot perceive another human being as a person, as an inward and unique consciousness. He does not perceive himself as a person either. In short, he has no conception of the meaning of personality—in others or in himself.

Inconsiderateness may be a small defect compared to more extreme and exaggerated forms. But inconsiderateness is the seed which, when fully grown, becomes the cruelty of war.

Crime is an exaggerated expression of this theory of humanity. For the criminal, the victim is a *thing* whose life is meaningless. The philosophical assumption some criminals make is that, just as a cow can be butchered for its meat, so can a citizen be butchered for the contents of his or her wallet. The criminal is ignorant of the fact that the presence of consciousness creates an aura of holiness that is never possessed by objects alone.

An even more exaggerated form of inconsiderateness is terrorism. The terrorist Kozo Okamoto, representing the Popular Front for the Liberation of Palestine, machine-gunned innocent Puerto Rican women and children pilgrims to the Holy Land at Lod International Airport in Tel Aviv in order, ultimately, to establish a new, Maoist, world order. "It is right," for Okamoto and in his own words, "to destroy other human beings for the sake of establishing a new world order in which people will forcefully be rearranged, programmed and reorganized for the sake of their own 'happiness'." And the nature of happiness is not defined by each individual subjectivity, but by Okamoto.

The final expression of cynical disregard for the integrity of individuals is war. War is possible solely because the populations of the warring nations live by a ghost-in-a-machine theory of humanity. No matter how nations and societies protest about their moral and ethical standing, they ultimately depend on war to achieve their goals. Our use of war as an instrument of policy presupposes our conviction that people are things (our own people as well as our enemy's). If the two cultures were based on a field-of-consciousness theory, empathy for individual subjectivities and sensitivity for the value and integrity of each living consciousness would take precedence over any killing and destruction. "Make love, not war," when translated into the language of philosophy, becomes "Recognize the truth of the field-of-consciousness theory of and the error of the ghost-in-a-machine theory of humanity."

2. A second consequence of having integrated the ghost-in-a-machine theory into the life of our society is that it has killed

love. It creates the inability to love by confusing love with the mechanics of sexual petting, physical manipulation, intercourse, and various perversions. It leads to the confusion of true love with role-playing that is thoroughly empty, shallow, energy-consuming, and eventually boring and unsatisfying.

Love is a meeting on the level of pure consciousness. In love, it is not two bodies that meet, nor is it two roles. In love, two inward subjectivities meet. That kind of meeting requires both to have access to and understanding of their subjective, inward consciousness. Love makes human beings complete. If I think of myself as a thing only—and think of others as things for manipulation only—then love is definitely not one of the joys to which I have access.

Love also means deciding to care for another. It means making a commitment *to* the other, for the welfare *of* the other. He who loves can say, "I have chosen to *care* about what happens to you because I see in you a true human inwardness and because I am also a human subjective consciousness." These insights make sense only in a field-of-consciousness theory of humanity; within the parameters of a ghost-in-a-machine theory they are incomprehensible and meaningless.

3. The ghost-in-a-machine theory, if integrated into life, results in the inability to communicate with others and share with them. Through the operation of a materialistic and object-oriented self-concept one loses the capacity to be *with* others. In the context of this theory, the only relation to people that is possible is one of manipulation for use, for profit, for individual advancement, and for the accumulation of power, status, and success.

Grayson is an advancing executive in the aerospace industry, personnel manager of the large research department of a western airplane and space equipment manufacturer. One morning Grayson had a choice to make: (1) visit and hold the hand of his six-year-old daughter, in the hospital after a routine tonsillectomy, or (2) please his boss by attending an important awards breakfast being held for the employees over whom he has jurisdiction.

To choose to be with his daughter meant to choose a meeting of two inwardnesses, perhaps through the touch of two hands. It would have been the meeting of the anxious, but loving consciousness of a father with the consciousness of his pained, lonely and speechless daughter, a meeting effected by a connecting glance or by the gentle touch of hands.

To choose to be with his boss meant an almost certain step toward further advancement. Attendance at the awards breakfast would have meant that Grayson pleased his boss, demonstrated his importance and his skill to the other employees, and participated in an important aspect of the company's personnel operations. Grayson's relationship with the child represents the field-of-consciousness theory, whereas the corporation in this context represents the ghost-in-a-machine theory in his life. Grayson's daughter represents the opportunity and the need for a caring consciousness-to-consciousness encounter. The reward for opening his consciousness to the encounter with another consciousness is the opportunity to communicate as well as to love and to be loved, an opportunity that only a consciousness can understand. On the other hand, Grayson's corporation represents the manipulation of people for personal advancement and success, the rewards of which are money, the satisfaction of the material needs of his family and the envy of others. Grayson's choice is between two self-concepts and their integration into his life. He must decide, not whether to go to the hospital or to the plant, but which of the two conflicting theories he is to make his own. His dilemma is philosophical and universal; it is not a small family or business decision.

Grayson chose the corporation.

4. A fourth consequence of the ghost-in-a-machine theory is the enslavement to roles found among people in all walks of life. As long as a person thinks of himself or herself as a thing, he or she believes the fulfillment of that thing to be found in being some specific role: it may be *his* manhood or *her* feminity. His role may be that of a tough-guy and gang leader or hers that of an ever-understanding and uncomplaining therapist. In a field-of-consciousness theory, every authentic

person must say to himself or herself, "What matters is that I am not my roles and that believing myself to be my roles destroys my potential for living."

A New York sociologist devised a simple exercise with a dual purpose — to tell us first what our actual roles are and then to show us how not to be enslaved by them. You can test yourself as follows: Log a record for one day only of all the roles and games you play during that day. Here is an example, produced by Lorne, a recent college graduate.

6:00 A.M. Asleep. Role of dreaming and total relaxation. Complete genuineness. Role of being a baby all over again. Deepest feelings are permitted to emerge.

7:30 A.M. Go to coffee shop for breakfast. Role of customer. Engage in business transaction and jovial small talk with waitress. My private thoughts are left behind.

8:00 A.M. Drive to work with Cliff and Mike. We talk about the latest sports scores, cars, office gossip, and vacations. I enjoy the role of male companionship, togetherness, in-group feeling, and brotherhood in the "male-talk" role.

8:30 A.M. I greet my boss. I am now in the role of employee. I try to act to impress him, because I may be in line for promotion. I quickly find my place in the status ladder and in the office organization and I attempt to fill that role perfectly. I want to be accepted in that role.

10:05 A.M. I flirt with Lola, the girl in the front office. She doubles as receptionist and telephone operator. I am now in the role of a "male on the make." I say those things which will give me Lola's attention and which will impress her. I show her how masculine, desirable, and considerate I am. I wear masculine clothes, make seductive allusions, and do her favors and express great sympathy and understanding.

12:15 P.M. I meet Mother for lunch. I slip into the role of the immature and whining son. I complain about my teeth, my job, and my apartment. I am a child and not an adult. I get moody and depressed. I am not particularly pleasant to Mother, nor am I interested in pleasing her. I am like a sloppy adolescent coming in for some morning breakfast.

2:25 P.M. We have a fire drill in the office building. I am in charge of evacuating the fifth floor. I now play the role of the captain or the commander, of hero, of leader, the dependable tough guy. I have "leadership" potential.

5:15 P.M. I fight the traffic in a rented car and I slip into the role of primitive "kill or be killed" behavior. I assume the role of a jungle animal, behaving in ways of which I will be ashamed later. I slip into the role of an irresponsible and pure instinct for self-seeking and self-preservation. I mistreat the rented car and ignore pedestrians and other drivers.

6:30 P.M. I go to *The Marina* for dinner. It is a fancy restaurant. I now play the role of the wealthy snob — I demand service and respect. I spend money as if it were water, tipping everyone and ordering the most expensive item on the menu. I fancy myself a wine connoisseur. I play the role of the aristocrat.

11:00 P.M. I go home and to bed, wishing I had Lola in my arms sleeping next to me. I dream of filling the role of a great lover. I return to the reveries of my unconscious, playing no role at all, or again, that of an infant who is prey solely to his instincts and his impulses.

This list is a record of the various roles Lorne plays in one day. If he understands the field-of-consciousness theory of humanity he knows that, while he *plays* all of these roles, in truth he *is* none of them. His true self is the consciousness that has, observes, entertains, or chooses these roles — not the roles themselves. The roles are objects to this consciousness; they are organizations of the data or objects of the world, and he is in danger of confusing his consciousness with these objects. The roles are things — sociological things; Lorne is not a thing, he is a consciousness. He is free. The roles are his in the same sense that the negative pole of a magnet *is* the positive pole of that magnet.

In the ghost-in-a-machine theory, Lorne *is* these roles. He is thus committed to play them out exactly as they are written by the demands of society. He is therefore a slave. If he should ever get used to this slavery, he will have lost the ability to recognize what is human in himself and in others. I believe that if the world continues to subscribe to the ghost-in-a-machine theory of humanity, the result will be the eventual elimination of humans from the face of the earth: not by ecological pollution or nuclear holocaust, but by philosophical misdefinition.

What is the practical point of knowing the difference between Lorne's real self and the roles that this self plays? Knowledge of the difference is freedom from the confusion, freedom from the enslaving consequences of identification. A person who has freed himself from the enslavement of roles can choose and change roles deliberately and rationally. In the case of Lorne, the following happened. As he became free from his slav sh identification with and dependency on his roles, he discovered that the role he really wanted was that of a scholar. For him this was the best reflection of the field that is his consciousness, creating a continuity of his inner consciousness with the practical world around him. His scholarship was an *expression* of consciousness onto the world and an incorporation of the world into consciousness. No other role fit his field of consciousness equally well.

He promptly resigned from his job and entered graduate school, specializing in Greek philology. That was a role deliberately and authentically chosen by his conscious inwardness. This authentic choice was possible only by having abandoned the ghost theory and having integrated into his manner of existing in the world the field-of-consciousness theory of humanity. Lorne has not regretted this decision.

5. Individuals who have completely integrated the ghost-in-a-machine theory into their lives will develop symptoms once the immediate gratifications have passed. They will feel that life is meaningless and that existence lacks purpose. As a result they will need more and more physical stimulation. They will turn more and more to titillations: overeating, alcohol, spending money on baubles, taking drugs, sexual perversions, violence—first in fantasy and then in reality. The final physical sensation may be murder, or suicide, or both. The escalation is inevitable. We live in a supersaturated culture whose insensitivity requires an ever-increasing violence of excitement. We have lost the sense of peace and silence and have succumbed to an exponentially growing fever of activity.

The person who knows that he or she is a field of consciousness will not search for increased physical sensations but will instead be able to rest peacefully and meaningfully in the security of inward consciousness and the joy that is the meeting of and caring for another consciousness. He or she will not seek pleasure and property exclusively, but will require primarily meaning and love.

6. People who think they are things have no self-confidence; they lack any sense of genuine independence. They cannot make decisions. They do not understand the meaning of being an individual, because they have no respect for uniqueness in themselves and in others. Moreover, they have no base of operations, no home, and no headquarters. They have all the attributes of a thing; they are hard, unfeeling, unloving, unresponsive, and not at peace. Self-confidence and independence are characteristics of consciousness only, never of things or objects. Self-reliance is a trait of a consciousness that is self-conscious, not of a thing that merely exists, is there, vegetates in its concreteness. Security and self-respect are the result of knowing the permanence, primacy, and indestructibility of consciousness. These strengths can never follow from being an object, because every object is finite and ephemeral. Only consciousness is experienced as a universal phenomenon.

7. The ghost-in-a-machine theory leads to imitation rather than creativity. The creative mind is a consciousness at work; it feels and expresses its nature. Consciousness is the act of freedom creating. The notion of creativity makes sense only within a philosophy of consciousness. Creativity as a human value can never be derived from the characteristics of objects. A thing is programmed and replicated; it has no possibility for originality. The artist, the inventor, the original thinker, and the innovator in all walks of life therefore are persons who know they are a *consciousness* and not a *thing*. They have integrated the field-of-consciousness theory into their being.

The person who believes that he or she is an object like an animal or a rock will never be able to produce a single original idea — that is, an idea, an act, a work of art, an invention, a business, or an institution which is a novel organization that springs into existence like the universe being created by God. That is why creativity can never be taught. It can only be un-covered, discovered, and experienced.

8. The ghost-in-a-machine theory of humanity has no room for freedom. Freedom is what makes us human, and if men and women are things, they are not free. If a man thinks of himself as a thing, he can have no respect for the institution of freedom in our society. A thing cannot respect the freedom of others because it does not discover freedom in itself. Further-more, such a man or woman is incapable of using freedom. The mark of an authentic society is that it holds freedom sa-cred above all; and the mark of an authentic person is that he or she unfailingly acts in accordance with the free nature that he or she is. Each assumes responsibility for life, can make choices and decisions. An authentic individual is proud of his or her freedom because it is the human essence. Only a field-of-consciousness theory allows for the unquestioned existence and the untarnished dignity of human freedom.

To say that human beings are things is to deny their free-dom and to spell the death of civilization. A free society will say to its members, "Each of you has the right to develop your life as you individually see fit." An unfree society will say, "We know what you should become, we know what is good for you, and we will force you to live accordingly."

A free human being can say, "I have decided to redefine myself from a person who *cannot* handle his problem job to a person who *can*." Greg hated his job as a supervisor in a can manufacturing company. It was an excellent job for an un-skilled laborer, but the personal working conditions were completely unacceptable to him. He could not quit because the money was good and he had three children and a pregnant wife to support. An economic recession was in full swing and no other jobs were available. His situation became intolerable. He could not choose to quit, nor could he choose to stay. Then he gradually learned the meaning of the fact that he *is* free. His true choice was between (1) "I am a man who *can* handle

this conflict" and (2) "I am a man who *cannot* handle this conflict." Up to now, Greg had chosen himself as a man who
could not handle the conflict between staying or quitting. He
had thought it was a *fact* that he could not handle the conflict.
How he knows he has a *choice*. He knows that there are two
types of people: those who can manage life as they find it and
those who cannot. He also knows that he chooses his own definition of who he is. Greg has discovered that he had defined
himself as a person who could *not* cope with life. He now took
personal responsibility for the decision which he tacitly had
made and lived, making it relatively easy to change that decision, because he saw that this choice of self-definition was not
inevitable.

Fortunately for Greg's wife and children, he chose to
redefine himself as a man who *can* handle the conflict, a man
who *can* cope with life. Once that decision was accomplished,
he was able to make a second choice—he decided to keep his
job, put up with it, and advance beyond it.

Within three months Greg was named manager of his divi-
sion.

We have examined the human consciousness using a number of helpful metaphors. The following statements, representing various existential themes, can now be seen to represent a person who is striving to live by a field-of-consciousness
concept of being.

1. I am neither a body nor a soul but a continuous consciousness-body-world field.
2. I choose myself as one who is realistically flexible.
3. I experience time as living in a present which, while
   utilizing the past, connects directly and primarily into my
   future.
4. My life is an endless process of growing, emerging, and
   reaching out.
5. There exists a consciousness within me which I am and
   which is eternal.
6. I always choose because I am always free.

7. As an adult I can choose to meet, confront, witness, understand, and be mirrored by another. I can also choose to love and care for that person.

Now we are ready to discuss two concepts of consciousness that shape our personality and our environment.

2

Two Concepts of Consciousness

Each of us has two self-concepts, or self-images. One is social and the other individual. Our *social* self-image is a cultural affair. The social self-concept is that aspect of our self-image which we all share as members of the human race and as partners in our community. It shapes our civilization, our political institutions, our religious ceremonies, the direction of our scientific and technological progress.

For example, our social self-concept tells us that "all men are created equal," and therefore we have a Bill of Rights which we expect the courts to implement. Our social self-concept tells us that progress is good, and therefore the technological revolution is permitted to advance unchecked and to destroy the balance of nature, as well as economic and social balances. Our social self-concept tells us that pride in our country is right, and therefore we are willing to fight wars. Our social self-concept tells us that advancement and success are positive values, and therefore we compete rather than cooperate, seek supremacy rather than compassion. Our social self-concept tells us that human beings are bodies rather than minds, and therefore we come to believe that a loving and caring encounter is achieved by the proper techniques of sexual manipulation. Furthermore, our social self-concept tells us that we *are* our bodies and that a young body is better than an old body. We accept and introject that idea and submit to much meaningless cosmetic manipulation in the vain hope that visually improving the body will lead to fulfillment in the mind.

Our *individual* self-concept is, on the other hand, a personal affair. Our individual self-concept is that aspect of ourselves which we do not share with others; it is that part which is exclusively and uniquely ours. Our individual self-image shapes our unique personality and our individualized lifestyle. An individual self-concept is a program that organizes our individual and private life.

An individual self-image, learned early in life and at a preconceptual level, may say "I am a failure." The seed that holds this self-image then grows into a total lifestyle. The individual with that self-image in his or her program will create situations which cleverly but invariably lead to failure. Janice, for instance, is always willing to take on another assignment — from the PTA, the teacher, her husband, the church membership committee, or the League of Women Voters. She automatically commits herself to tasks that are too numerous and too difficult for her to handle. She makes these commitments, unconsciously to be sure, in order to assure failure. Her failure program governs her life. We can, as a result, predict her behavior by it.

Another popular individual self-concept is "I am your servant." The perennial servant will never be assertive, will always be timid, will allow himself or herself to be used by others. The "servant" will never take his or her own legitimate claims seriously. Walter, ever since he can remember, has had an overwhelming need to be popular. He ascertains what others want, then does it for them and in return expects their gratitude. He wants to please his boss, his wife, his parents, and his teachers. He would have made an excellent butler, albeit somewhat demanding of approval. But he forgets throughout to please himself. Everyone likes Walter — but he is soon forgotten and he is certainly ignored when assignments require a well-developed sense of responsibility and a mature sense of leadership. Walter is the victim of an individual self-concept implanted early into his personality. His health and self-respect require that he change that self-image.

Richard's self-image consists of a different program. It reads "You are attacking me." Richard is therefore always aggressively on the defensive. He is distrustful, hostile, and unpleasant because he responds, not to the real person he meets, but to the attacker he has invented. He fabricates reasons for his behavior such as "You do not recognize my skill," or "You are not paying adequate attention to me," or "I need no one; I am fully independent." But the true reason for his aggressiveness is in the program of his self-image. As a result of that distorted self-image, Richard makes all those around him miserable and creates an armed camp rather than a loving home as his environment.

How can you tell what your individual self-concept is? There exists a simple but effective procedure. Take a good objective look at your life—perhaps with the help of a trusted friend. Now comes the crucial point. Make the assumption that you brought about your relations with people and your lifestyle deliberately. Tell yourself "I created my world. I created my personality and I am responsible for my personality. I created my social relations and I am responsible for them. I constructed my environment; I alone am responsible for my environment and only I can change my environment." A general rule is that your individual world—personal, social, and environmental—is a strong clue to your self-image. If you are, let us say, twenty-five years old, you may assume that for at least twenty of those years your self-concept has functioned as a guidance system to direct your perceptions of the world.

After ten years of no philosophical reflection at all, Sally finds herself in a marriage that offers her no opportunity for fulfillment. She is far better educated than Varner, her husband. Furthermore, Sally is dependent, open, and loving, while her husband is closed and independent. In addition, Varner is cruel and Sally resents but accepts his cruelty. If Sally now admits to herself that she married Varner precisely so that she could suffer—and it is not only painful but also requires strength and courage to make that admission—then she will have a clue to the individual self-concept that works within her like a hidden program. Sally's self-concept is "I must be punished. I must remain forever unfulfilled. I do not deserve a happy life." She may discover that self-concept by deliberately assuming total responsibility for the life she is leading. Then she will be ready to eliminate her self-destructive patterns.

If we wish to improve the quality of our lives, we must discover the self-concept that causes the trouble and exchange it for one that will produce the life we want and deserve. It is here that philosophy can fulfill its promise of compassion for the suffering of mankind. Just as a healthy and honest self-concept enables an individual to have a healthy and fulfilled life, the self-concept of a society can influence its behavior. Our culture today is governed by a dangerous and dehumanizing self-concept. If we replace it with a new one that is healthy and accurate, we can change our individual lives from despair to joy and the life of our society from alienation to brotherhood—and even begin to turn from war to peace. Because consciousness creates our individual and our world image, consciousness can also change the images, from destructive to constructive ones, from stale ones to creative ones, and from pained to joyous world views.

Conflicting Self-Concepts

Let us begin the analysis of the conflict between an authentic and an inauthentic self-concept by looking at two entirely different, in fact sharply opposed, opinions on what love—a deep relationship between two human beings—really is. Lynn, a recent college graduate and an aspiring young actress who is working in a Los Angeles restaurant-club while taking dancing and acting lessons, writes about meeting one of America's most famous actors.

Dear Dr. Koestenbaum:

I had quite an unusual experience last night. Mr. X is a frequent customer in the restaurant I work in. He's _____ years old, is extremely intelligent, quite wealthy and has a heart condition that the public knows nothing about and, thus, feels time is rapidly running out. We had a long talk; he wanted to know about me— asked me a lot about myself, informed me that he is nothing *but* honest and because time is an important element, he objects violently to any sort of game-playing. Now, to get to the heart of this, he wants my "company" a couple nights a week.—to have conversation etc., and sex would be a part of it—*but* he *emphatically* informed me he would *never force* me to do anything I didn't want—we did *not* have to have intercourse. Wow, he said he realized I needed to get *something* out of a situation like this. He said he would give me a couple hundred dollars a week. He would also help me out anyway he was able to—career-wise.

As I sat there and listened, I was astounded that *I* was listening to all of this and it was happening to me. This man has studied psychology in school and is constantly reading this type of material. I may add he is an avid believer in *Freud*. And, he has two double sessions with what he called a "shrink" a week. So he used his "psychological" background on me. He told me if I agreed with this setup I would grow fantastically from the knowledge I could learn from him on life, The Business—and other miscellaneous bullshit.

I felt he was using tricks on me that his psychiatrist uses on him: his trying to reveal something shocking to me about myself. He embarked on an extensive monologue telling me how he could help me overcome my "hangups" or whatever. I said this was not the type of situation in which I would even *attempt* to iron out what problems I *may* have! I restated that I *could not* become sexually involved with him. Then, he pointed out the benefits again: 1. money, 2. knowledge I could gain, and 3. his helping me become free. Oh yes, he told me I was *not* free. That I was restricting myself. He then told me there was three hundred dollars in my purse which he had put there when I left the room to go to the ladies' room—he thought I would probably agree to his proposition and he didn't like the money end of it—so he secretively put it in my purse.

Notice the contrasting view of love expressed by the late British philosopher and mathematician, Lord Bertrand Russell. His poem is dedicated to the one who was probably his last love and it is in the original handwriting, the frontispiece to the first volume of his *Autobiography**:

---

* *The Autobiography of Bertrand Russell* (Boston: Little, Brown and Co., 1967), p. 4.

To Edith

Through the long years
   I sought peace.
I found ecstasy, I found anguish,
   I found madness,
I found loneliness.
I found the solitary pain
   that gnaws the heart,
But peace I did not find.

Now, old and near my end,
   I have known you,
And, knowing you,
I have found both ecstasy and peace.
   I know rest,
After so many lonely years.
I know what life and love may be—
Now, if I sleep
I shall sleep fulfilled.

The episode with X in Lynn's letter is based on the view that happiness consists of manipulating objects, and that human beings are things meant expressly to be used for gratification. Women are sex-things and men are sex-machines. Love is a purchased physical titillation: It is a commodity that can be bought with money, with the allure of advancement, the temptation of widened experience, and the promise of sheer pleasure. The assumption is that fulfillment and contentment in life can be achieved through this materialistic view.

When Bertrand Russell speaks of love it is entirely different. He refers to human inwardness, to the peaceful conscious center. He refers to values and beauties that can be understood only by a human subjectivity and not by anything developing out of the objective animal organism. He most emphatically does not refer to people as bodies, things, organisms, or objects. He recognizes that the first nature of a human being is to be a conscious subjectivity, an inward ego. And that ego is pure awareness, pure inwardness, and is not a material object of any kind. This contrasting view of human nature—that the essence of humanity is first consciousness and not merely body—is the *field-of-consciousness theory* of humanity. The view that we are a subjective consciousness first and a material body in a natural world second is the *field theory* or the *field-of-being theory* of humanity.

Our culture is the incarnation of the ghost-in-a-machine theory of humankind. It has fully integrated into its operations the conviction that we are things, that our values are the values of things, and that our goals are the goals of things. The effect of assimilating this materialistic and objectivistic opinion of ourselves into our personal lives and into our society in general amounts to no less than the death of civilization itself. The human-being-is-a-thing theory is at the root of the destruction of all our specifically human values, such as character, integrity, freedom, reason and compassion. The ghost-in-a-machine theory leads to totalitarianism and authoritarianism in both our personal relations and the political institutions of our society. If people are things, then violence and tyranny are but the natural manifestations of the desire to rearrange objects (people) for the sake of a superior social order (happiness). Disrespect for inwardness is the badge of the tyrant and the license of the bureaucrat.

On the personal level, the ghost theory, when applied to daily living, can express itself, especially at the onset of middle age, in boredom and a sense of meaninglessness. The same malaise can afflict a society; it is afflicting the United States at this time. We are a society at middle age, incapable of handling the philosophic problem of meaninglessness. We seek additional technology when what we need is deeper understanding of ourselves.

If an engine needs new pistons, the broken ones are discarded and new ones installed in their place. What matters to the mechanic is not the fate of the broken pistons but the success of the engine. If we believe people are things then we treat them like pistons. When their needs interfere with the smooth operation of society we relegate them to jail or hospital, because what matters is the progress of society and not the rights of the individual. And the idea of rights makes no sense to one who thinks people are objects. The concept of rights can be understood only in the framework of a field-of-consciousness theory of humanity.

In the last analysis, the ghost-in-a-machine theory could ultimately force us to condone the destruction of crippled children and the infirm aged because their utility to society has ceased. Only the philosophical recognition that each person possesses—or *is*—a conscious inwardness can save individuals from insensitivity and indifference and our society from the barbarism toward which it is headed.

The mechanization of humanity is perhaps most dangerous in that noble profession, medicine. Yet the pervasive influence of the ghost-in-a-machine theory in medicine is often almost beyond belief. Gerry, a Ph.D. in biophysics and molecular biology from one of the nation's most prestigious universities, was working for his second doctorate, in psychiatry, when he wrote to me:

I am presently studying in almost total seclusion for the Medical College Admission Test I am required to take in two weeks. It involves mostly refreshing my memory with all the intricate details of general biology, chemistry, and physics, as well as little-used English vocabulary. Questions on existential philosophy, phenomenology, or even just meaningful questions in humanistic areas are certainly not represented on this test that examines the preparation of our future doctors. Instead they ask questions such as which of four obscure reagents is best for separating cadmium from copper ions or what number the product of the specific heat and atomic weight is for metals.

Philosophy leads to health (in persons and in society) because it changes our views from a ghost-in-a-machine theory to a field-of-consciousness theory of humanity and because that change in self-concept leads to new persons, to new relations among people and a new social order.

Many Americans saw a dreadful and terrifying NBC television program on July 28, 1972. It was an hour-long interview with two Utah convicts: Walter Kelbach and Myron Lance. These two men recounted how together in a short time they knifed and shot to death six people. They represent the ultimate in the degeneration that follows from refusing to recognize and be sensitive to the subjective, conscious inwardness of other human beings.

The essentials the interview disclosed about the criminals were these:

1. They were sane, legally and psychiatrically. Two psychologists testified to that.

2. They were on pills and beer but nevertheless aware of what they were doing. The drugs facilitated the acting out of their impulses and fantasies. They *wanted* to kill. They took the drugs voluntarily, to help themselves do what they wanted to do.

3. The murder spree was a joyful experience. They delighted in terrifying, killing, shooting, and knifing innocent victims and were amused by their success in evading the police.

4. In recounting the crimes, they found great humor in some of the horror situations they created and in their victims' panic, bargaining, and prayers. Sadism was part of their joy; a typical comment was made by Lance as he recalled his knifing of a gas station attendant: "He was gagging on his blood, and it just hit me kind of funny. So I got him with the knife and he quit his gagging."

5. The lifelong possession and use of knife and gun gave them a sense of power, worth, dignity, respectability, and significance. The world recognized their existence and the weapons gave them enormous freedom of movement (space and time) in the world.

6. The enjoyed greatly the newspaper and television publicity.

7. Their background, family and personal, was one of total violence.

8. They experienced no remorse, regret, or pity for any of their victims nor for the orphans that they created.

The crucial point is the final item — the inability to feel pity for their victims. A person who has the capacity for empathy and pity will refrain from crime.

What is missing in a person who lacks a sense of compassion? The answer is simple — compassion is possible only if we know that a human being is a conscious inwardness, a subjective center, an experiencing ego, and not just a body or mass of protoplasm that is disposable and replaceable. One source of the criminal mentality is total ignorance of the conscious nature of any and every person. A clear knowledge and perception of the inwardness of potential victims will make it distasteful to hurt them. In failing to recognize the consciousness of the victim, the criminal also fails to perceive the existence of his or her own consciousness. Kelbach and Lance were not mentally ill — they were philosophically ignorant. And our society today is in danger of a similar gross ignorance!

There are basically only three explanations for criminal acts: insanity, philosophical ignorance, or deliberate and free choice. The two men in question were sane. Their crimes are therefore due either to gross philosophical ignorance — that is, ignorance about the field of consciousness, ignorance about human subjectivity and of its holy nature — or they are due to a deliberate choice of denying that philosophical insight. They are thus either ignorant or evil. If they are ignorant they must be taught and if they are evil they must be punished. However, the expression "must be taught" refers to more than mere verbal repetition; it means integration into the personality. By the time middle age is reached, reteaching in this sense may be impossible. But I hope not, and I have chosen to live and act on that hope.

The controversial book and film *A Clockwork Orange* described a society in which both criminals and the Establishment reflect the thorough application of the ghost-in-a-machine theory of humanity. Criminals and ministers of justice, murderers and law-enforcement officers become indistinguishable. And the cure for crime in *Clockwork Orange,* as in any society based on this theory, is reconditioning. The reconditioned and "rehabilitated" felon has not lost his free will.

But whenever the sexual and criminal urges surface in the character his body becomes violently ill. His subjectivity has not been affected, but his options for action have been severely limited. His body has been modified. After behavior modification, the criminal, being human, is subjectively as free as he was before. The difference now is that he is jailed, not behind prison bars, but inside his reconditioned body.

3

The Master Outline

The Master Table presented in this chapter is a carefully constructed, formalized statement of those aspects of our human existence that need to be known and applied in order to lead an authentic life. The scores on the test exercise associated with it are, of course, in no way as important as the activity. By taking the test exercise, you will be compelled to think about the basics of the existential personality theory. Also, by comparing your own life to these existential ideals, you will become aware of the extent to which you think that you are a mature and authentic individual. New perspectives on life may be opened in this manner.

Each theme in the test exercise consists of four parts. First, you will find a brief expression or a simple word that characterizes a particular theme of the existential personality theory. Second, you are given a sentence that has been carefully constructed to summarize a considerable amount of existential research into the nature of man and thus to present an ideal human condition as well. Third, you will find an explanatory paragraph discussing the philosophic meaning of each one of these themes. Finally you will find the abbreviation for that theme as it is used on the profile (such as Li for Life). You will also notice that the test exercise is divided into three main sections: *The nature, the rule, and the principles* of human existence.

The Master Table can be a subjective evaluation of the extent to which you understand and use existential philosophy in your life. Do this exercise twice, now and after you finish this book and have had a chance to reflect on its contents. The significance of your score lies not in its absolute value but in the change that occurs from the first to the second time, or any other time, you do the exercise. It is also interesting and insightful to examine the relation between your understanding and your opinion on how you use that understanding.

Instructions

Answer the following two questions about each of the nineteen (19) themes of the Master Table. Be slow, careful and thoughtful. Plan to spend more than an hour on the test exercise and feel free to pause occasionally.

Question I. *"To what extent do I agree intellectually with the idea, statement or concept?"* Choose your answers from among the following alternatives:

0.	I do not understand the idea.
10.	I do *not* agree *at all.*
20.	I agree *very little.*
30.	I agree to a *reasonable* extent.
40.	I agree *very much.*
50.	I agree *almost completely.*
60.	I agree *totally, enthusiastically* and *without reservations.*

```
 |____|_____|_____|_____|_____|_____|____|
 0    10     20     30     40     50     60
```

Question II. *"How often do I use this idea, statement, or concept in my life? How often do I find that this idea is integrated into my style of life? How accurately does the concept describe me as I truly am?"* Choose your answers from among the following alternatives:

0.	Since I do not understand the idea, I do not know if I apply it.
10.	I *never* apply it. I *never* am like that.
20.	I *rarely* apply it. I *rarely* am like that.
30.	I *occasionally* apply it. I *occasionally* am like that.
40.	I *frequently* apply it. I *frequently* am like that.

50. I apply it *most of the time.* I am like that *most of the time.*
60. I apply it *always* and *enthusiastically.* I am like that *always* and *enthusiastically.*

Answer according to the following directions: Mark an X in the appropriate place of the scale. After you have made all your marks, translate each mark into a number. For example:

| 0 | 10 | 20 | 30 | 40 | 50 | 60 | becomes 30 |

| 0 | 10 | 20 | 30 | 40 | 50 | 60 | becomes 35 |

| 0 | 10 | 20 | 30 | 40 | 50 | 60 | becomes 23 |

| 0 | 10 | 20 | 30 | 40 | 50 | 60 | becomes 17 |

Use the answer sheets that appear at the end of the Master Table.

The Master Table

This is a summary of the insights about the nature of humanity developed by a hundred years of existential philosophy. The outline is carefully formulated to emphasize the practical application of existential philosophy.

Read carefully. The subsequent discussion and case histories will explain the meanings of these insights.

A.   The *Nature* of Human Existence
   1. *The Field Theory of Humanity.* "*I am neither a body nor a soul but a continuous consciousness-body-world field.*"
   Explanation: I do not exist in isolation. I am one with

other people and one with nature. Whatever affects other
people and the environment also affects me, and whatever
happens to me affects other people and the world around me.
(FT)

2. *The Two Selves.* "*I am a pure consciousness with a
psychological personality, a physical body, and many social
roles.*"

Explanation: I am more than just a body and even more
than a personality. I am also a pure consciousness or a pure
awareness that is different from the person that is known by
my name and my likeness. I am a center, the depths of which
only I can plumb. (TS)

2a. *Four Modes of Consciousness.* "*Consciousness can be
experienced as either individual, intimate, cosmic, or as an
Eternal Now.*"

Explanation: I understand that there is much confusion
about the nature of the ego, because different cultures have
different definitions of what it means to be a self. I am willing
to experience at least four separate ways in which the consciousness that runs through me can manifest itself in me.

The first, and most common, is the experience of consciousness as being an individual. Individual consciousness is
the center of all my experiences. Individual consciousness feels
comfortable with itself but isolated from other people and
from the world of nature.

I am also an intimate consciousness. I can experience complete oneness with another person. There exists a perceptible
connecting conscious space between me and another person. I
can perceive the center of another person directly; I can also
sense how another experiences my center directly.

Third, I can experience the fact that I am part of a cosmic
conscious stream and that I share and participate fully in the
endless processes of nature. I am a wave in an ocean of consciousness. I have the same boundaries as empty space-time.

The final, and deepest, level in which consciousness mani-
fests itself is what can be called the Eternal Now. In it, even
space-time becomes an object to consciousness. The Eternal

Now as the source of consciousness is experienced to be outside of space and time. A psychic distance has been inserted between the ego as the Eternal Now and its most primitive objects, empty space and time. (MC)

3. *Responsibility.* "*I have created and am responsible for the organization of my world. I did not create the raw materials, but I am fully and alone responsible for the social reality that I have constructed around me and the lifestyle that I have organized for myself.*"

Explanation: If I am happy and successful it is not fate or luck but my own efforts and decisions that have led to my well-being. If I fail and am unhappy, then I am prepared to assume full responsibility for my problems. I feel that my problems are my own creations because I am in charge of my life — no one else is. It is good news to know that I help shape both the good and the bad in the world in which I live. I am prepared to fulfill my obligations. (Rs)

B.   The *Rule* for a Meaningful Human Existence

1. *Self-disclosure.* "*I must be fully disclosed to myself both as a human being and as* _____" (*write your name in this space*).

Explanation: I am excited at the thought of both therapy and philosophy. I look forward to exploring the person that I am. I anticipate with pleasure examining my feelings and attitudes. I want to study my personality and my body. I am also determined to understand the philosophical nature of humankind. I recognize the importance of questions regarding human destiny and about the meaning of life. I also appreciate the significance of morality. I consider these questions fundamental to a free and healthy life. (SD)

C.   The Sixteen *Principles* for Authentic Human Existence

1. *Pain.* "*I choose to value my pains.*"

Explanation: Suffering can be a learning experience. Pain is unavoidable. Death is a natural part of life. Anxiety and depression help me to understand the meaning of life. I can successfully cope with the fact that evil is an integral part of life. (P)

2. *Death.* "*I choose to value my limitations.*"

Explanation: I can adapt myself to frustrations. I know that much of the time I cannot have what I want. I know that over a lifetime I will be forced to give up many of my most cherished dreams. I am successful in accepting that which cannot be helped. I can accept the fact that all life ends in death. (D)

3. *Reflection.* "*I am able both to live my life and to reflect on my life.*"

Explanation: There are times when I am active and extroverted. I participate in life and I am involved. There are also times at which I am withdrawn and reflective—that is, introverted. If I so choose, I can meditate and be happy just being by myself and inside myself. I have control over these feelings and attitudes. They are usually appropriate to the circumstances of my life. (Rf)

4. *Self-reliance.* "*I am an adult consciousness that exists alone: I choose to be independent and self-reliant.*"

Explanation: I have outgrown childish forms of dependency. I can be comfortable being alone. I can go through life on my own two feet. I can take care of myself—and of others if necessary. I feel that this independence and self-reliance is an attitude that I voluntarily choose and not one that is imposed upon me from the outside. (SR)

5. *Individuality.* "*It is right and normal for me to seem different from other human beings.*"

Explanation: I am free to conform or not to confrom as my value system dictates. I am not excessively bothered by the fact that I may be different from my peers. I am prepared to create my own direction and my own life, one that I know is right for me even though it may differ from the prevailing lifestyles of those around me. I am not easily pressured by my associates and relatives. Neither am I easily pressured by my neighbors, by people that I meet, or by those who try to sell me something. (I)

6. *Eternity.* *"There exists a consciousness within me which I am and which is eternal."*

Explanation: This point is perhaps the most difficult one to understand. It means that I have a genuine conception and perception of my most inner inwardness. I have a real sense of the center that I am within me amidst the storms, stresses, and changes of life. I understand what wise persons of all ages mean when they refer to the pure consciousness within me that I am. I also recognize the universality of that center. The conscious center that I am is not susceptible to the flux of life and is therefore unchanging and timeless. It may not last forever, but it is outside of time. (E)

6a. *Reverence.* *"Each individual human inward subjectivity is the divine consciousness in that person."*

Explanation: Reverence for subjectivity is the highest existential principle of morality. A person's character may be evil or body diseased, but his or her pure inner conscious core is infinitely precious and eternally dignified. A person's inwardness is the source of his or her value; that inmost center is the foundation for the "unalienable rights of life, liberty, and the pursuit of happiness" with which each individual, according to the American Declaration of Independence, is born.

I am capable of respecting the inner ego of myself and of others. I can "hate the sin rather than the sinner." I agree with Maritain when he says "the true connection among people is spiritual." (Rv)

7. *Freedom.* *"I always choose because I am always free."*

Explanation: I have a realistic sense of the profound meaning of human freedom. I believe in the existence of free will. I believe that I am responsible for my actions and for my life. I believe that I set my own values and self-concepts and I am prepared to accept the full consequences. I am able to make decisions even while I realize that in most situations there are no definite truths and falsehoods, rights and wrongs. (F)

8. *Life.* *"My first and last choice is to say 'yes' to life."*

Explanation: If I say *yes* to life I recognize that I am fully responsible for whatever optimism or pessimism runs through my existence. If I am depressed *I* have said *no* to life. If I live with joy it is because *I* have said *yes* to life. If I say *yes* to life I freely choose to make living itself the highest value. In short, whether I love life or not, whether I am a positive or a negative personality is my own free personal choice for which I am fully responsible. I cannot blame others for my depression, anger, guilt or lack of self-respect. (Li)

9. *Commitment. "I am free to make commitments."*

Explanation: Commitment means that I feel connected with the world. I feel one with my body and one with the society and environment into which as a human being I am born. Commitment means that I can risk attachments to people, principles, goals, and lifestyles. I can take it if I lose. Commitment means that I can live as a full-fledged participant in the affairs of society and of the natural environment. My life is experienced whole rather than fragmented. (Cm)

9a. *Reality. "I clearly distinguish reality from fantasies, dreams, rationalizations and wishful thinking. I am always in touch with what is real."*

Explanation: I have a well-developed sense of reality. Even though I understand that the distinction between dream and reality is philosophically ambiguous, I find no difficulty separating dream from reality in my daily and practical life. I know that there is a reality beyond my inwardness. I know that this reality is different from my subjective ego. I know that this reality may be other people or the objects of nature, but it can also be my body or my unconscious (as I see in cases of physical or mental illness). I know that this reality is independent of me: sometimes it joins me in my needs and wishes, sometimes it is indifferent, and sometimes it opposes me. Nevertheless, at all times I feel that I am directly in touch with that external reality. I always sense that I am in contact with that part of the world which is other than me. Even while I am rationalizing, deceiving myself, or having fantasies, I know that what is real is that I am dreaming. (Rl)

10. *Love. "As an adult I can choose to meet, confront, witness, understand, and be mirrored by another. I can also choose to love him and care for him."*

Explanation: I am capable of loving like an adult. I can love spiritually and I can love physically. I do not use love neurotically. In love I can accept the dignity and the needs of my partner in love. If I so choose, I am able to make love the central project in my life. I enjoy spiritual, emotional, and physical love and love is easy and natural for me. (Lv)

11. *Adaptability.* "*I choose myself as one who is realistically flexible.*"

Explanation: I can be reflective and inward or active and outgoing, depending on my own choices and the circumstances in which I find myself. I can be self-reliant and independent if I want to but I also can be dependent and trusting if I choose that personality structure. I can be both a leader and a follower, as my decisions and the world's circumstances dictate. (A)

12. *Time.* "*I experience time as living in a present which, while utilizing the past, connects directly and primarily into my future.*"

Explanation: I experience my life as a continuous progression. My sense of time is not fragmented. My focus is on the future. I live in the present and I realize that both past and future are connected to me in the present. The burdens of the past exist for me in the present. The hopes and opportunities for the future exist for me in the present. I experience the time of my life as a river that flows always and smoothly in the direction of the future. (T)

13. *Growth.* "*My life is an endless process of growing, emerging and reaching out.*"

Explanation: For me, to live is to grow. I am not satisfied with achievements in life. My concern is rather with process and movement in my life. The meaning of my life is found in continual growth—in education, in human relationships, in occupational progress, in creativity, in building, and so forth. I feel that if my growing should end so would the meaning of my life. I know that either hate or disinterest are the results of a reaching out that has been frustrated. (G)

14. *Contradiction.* "*The inescapable ambiguities and contradictions of life are my powerful allies.*"

Explanation: When faced with contradictions in life I am not upset; instead, I am challenged. I realize that values and situations are usually ambiguous and unclear. There are many sides to most issues. I feel no compulsion always to discover the absolute right. I can act in spite of uncertainty. I can make decisions in spite of ambiguities. I can make commitments without being certain of the truth. I can tolerate disagreement, opposition, rejection, and denial. In fact, contradictions are to me a source of strength, because I find polarities within myself. I can integrate the polar opposites in me and achieve a mature sense of wholeness. (Cd)

ANSWER SHEET

Name _____ Question I_____ *Numerical equivalent*

0 10 20 30 40 50 60	
A1 (FT)	A1 ____
A2 (TS)	A2 ____
A3 (Rs)	A3 ____
B (SD)	B ____
C1 (P)	C1 ____
C2 (D)	C2 ____
C3 (Rf)	C3 ____
C4 (SR)	C4 ____
C5 (I)	C5 ____
0 10 20 30 40 50 60	
C6 (E)	C6 ____
C6a (Rv)	C6a ____
C7 (F)	C7 ____
C8 (Li)	C8 ____
C9 (Cm)	C9 ____
C10 (Lv)	C10 ____
C11 (A)	C11 ____
C12 (T)	C12 ____
C13 (G)	C13 ____
C14 (Cd)	C14 ____

Total _____

0 10 20 30 40 50 60

A2a (MC)
C9a (Rl)   (Statistics not available for these two scales)

43

ANSWER SHEET

Name _____ Question II _____

Numerical equivalent

| | | | | | | | |
0 10 20 30 40 50 60

A1 (FT)
A2 (TS)
A3 (Rs)

B (SD)

C1 (P)
C2 (D)
C3 (Rf)
C4 (SR)
C5 (I)

0 10 20 30 40 50 60

C6 (E)
C6a (Rv)
C7 (F)
C8 (Li)
C9 (Cm)
C10 (Lv)

C11 (A)
C12 (T)
C13 (G)
C14 (Cd)

A1 ___
A2 ___
A3 ___

B ___

C1 ___
C2 ___
C3 ___
C4 ___
C5 ___

C6 ___
C6a ___
C7 ___
C8 ___
C9 ___
C10 ___

C11 ___
C12 ___
C13 ___
C14 ___

Total _____

| | | | | | | | |
0 10 20 30 40 50 60

A2a (MC) (Statistics not available for these two scales)
C9a (Rl)

44

4

Interpreting Your Authenticity Profile

Now you can plot your scores on the profile sheets provided on page 58. Transfer your numerical score for each of the nineteen existential themes to the appropriate point on the profile. (In plotting your graph, note that items A2a and C9a are not on the profile blank. Because these themes were added late, no statistics for them exist.) You must exercise caution: The vertical interval between numbers is not the same from scale to scale; it is therefore necessary to interpolate approximately. For example, the numerical interval from average to above average on the FT scale (Question I) is from 43 to 56 so this distance is represented by 13 points. A score of 49 or 50, for instance, would then be plotted halfway between average and above average. However, on the E scale, the corresponding distance is represented by 20 points. Also, the order of the scales on the profile is not the same as in the test, so after C2 you will find C14 rather than C3.

When all the dots are in place, connect them to get a graph, as you will see in the samples.

The numbers that you use to plot your answers to QI appear *above* the horizontal lines, whereas the numbers needed to plot the answers to QII appear *below* these same horizontal lines. In this manner, maximum information can be incorporated in one profile sheet.

The vertical bars on the left of the profile sheet should be filled in to the level of the *totals* corresponding, respectively, to your answers to QI, QII, and to the difference between them. You might wish to consult the sample profiles included for further clarification.

What can be accomplished with these profiles? We get a better look at the inside of a human being. From then on we proceed intuitively, in the spirit of "Let's talk together about how the world looks to you from your vantage point."

A minor warning is in order. The discussion of profile interpretation may be slightly more esoteric than the other material in this book. To take the Master Table test exercise is a significant value in itself. To interpret it in accordance with the principles discussed in the next sections is not necessary.

Let me make a few observations about the profile in general.

Between the T-scores of 40 and 60 fall some 68 percent of those charted. Fourteen percent of the population falls between the T-scores of 60 and 70, and 14 percent between the T-scores of 30 and 40. Above 70 you find the upper 2 percent of the population—which for this test does not have any statistical meaning—and below 30, the bottom 2 percent.

The table is divided into three major sections: the summary section, the world-view section, and the anthropology section. The summary section provides an overview of the data. The world-view section is related to the general world view of existentialism. The last section concerns itself with our being-in-the-world; we might say that it deals with our emotional existence.

You must remember the *tentative character* of the profile. It is true that most subjects who take this test are very serious about their work. They seem to reflect thoughtfully on their answers and try to think of examples before deciding on a response. And it is rather common for subjects to spend two hours on the test. Nevertheless, *there is only one item,* one question, for each philosophic theme. That is not enough of a sample to yield statistically significant measures for your answer. But it is enough to stimulate serious thinking about your own authenticity. Also keep in mind that the standard for this test was developed from reasonably sophisticated adults enrolled in philosophy classes or in upper-division university courses. Standards for the general population are not available, but would perhaps be quite different.

Always remember that this test is a *totally subjective measure* of your subjectivity. It is not an objective, behavioral test. Like a mirror, it reflects to you and to others a picture of *how it feels to be you.* The test does that by comparing your subjective feelings with parallel intuitions of others. The test is an attempt to come as close as possible to the incredibly difficult task of comparing subjective intuitions. But you must live with yourself and you must live your own life. For the point of view of existential authenticity it is not as important to compare yourself to external standards or to the visible behavior of others as it is to understand your own inwardness.

The profile shows how philosophy can be used to help you understand yourself, to help you perceive yourself with increased sensitivity. It shows you how to use existential concepts and values for the sake of comprehending who you are.

The first examples are profiles in which only the answers to QII are plotted. The meaning of QI will be considered later. In order to interpret the meaning of your profile, you must be alert to the following features.

1. Examine its general pattern. Is it high or low? Consistent or inconsistent? Jane's profile is both high and consistent. Anything much higher than that might be artificial—that is, not answered openly and honestly. Mahlon's profile tends to be low and inconsistent. It has high and low points scattered throughout. In addition, it has high and low points in each of the subcategories or areas, especially encounter and survival.

2. Examine each individual area. Ask yourself, "Is it high?" "Is it low?" "Is it consistent?" and "How does it compare to other areas?" If the score in an area is high it would indicate a strength, an asset, in that area. For example, Jane is strong in accepting and integrating the negativities of life (Suffering). Mahlon is somewhat weak in the area of free will and Marilyn tends to be weak in the area of inwardness. Mark, who is strong in the areas of survival, free will, and suffering, can use those strengths to enhance his encounter and self-disclosure (he is low in both of these areas). Marilyn, who is strong in ontology and methodology, the area of world view, has an existential outlook on life. That strength can be the foundation

for raising her low self-respect (as shown by her low inwardness score). A note of caution is in order: Be wary of excessively high scores. In this test that would mean most scores just under a T-score of 70. The possibility always suggests itself that high scores are intellectual, defensive, and artificial. That is a suspicion worth exploring further.

3. Examine the QII and Difference scores. The Difference score can be interpreted variously as follows. A low score can mean self-satisfaction, a relaxed and unambitious personality. It can also mean stiffness, repression, and blindness about oneself. In general, a low Difference score seems to indicate a closed mind. It means the individual will not continue to grow. It also means a condition of hopelessness. A high score can mean motivation for self-development, the existence of meanings and goals in life. It can also mean guilt and a sense of inadequacy. In general, a high score means that the individual is open and eager for personalized philosophic work. He has hope.

Let us examine the question, "Do you perceive yourself as an authentic person?" Jane clearly does. Her QII score is above average. Her Difference score is above average notwithstanding the fact that QII is high already. The large difference between the conception of her ideal (QI) and the perception of her actual life or being-in-the-world (QII) does not come through to her as despair or guilt but as challenge, as the task that is giving meaning to her life.

Beth does not perceive herself as authentic. That can be seen in her extremely low QII score. In her case, the large Difference score is probably experienced by her as guilt and shame and is thus likely to come across as more of a burden than an incentive.

4. Examine the SD score. You are really answering the following kind of question: "Do you use the phenomenological method, the method of careful and sensitive, assumption-free, and introspective descriptions in the emotional and feeling aspects of your life?" A low SD score may mean repression or

lack of commitment to the task of a personalized philosophy, a philosophy of life, or a philosophy of humanity. It may mean that this task is unnecessary or irrelevant to the subject. On the other hand, a high score on that item may mean serious commitment to a lived philosophy. The score is only one response to one question; it is nevertheless significant. Even a low score is meaningful, because it was produced by an individual who, with considerable self-sacrifice, has enrolled in a course or a workshop and made a commitment to an arduous program of just the kind of philosophic self-development indicated by that question. He has with that commitment expressed his seriousness about the project of self-disclosure. A low score would still indicate serious and above-average commitment to philosophic and personal self-disclosure, at least in relation to the rest of the population.

5. Study your ontology score. How close to the existential model is your living world view? How close are you to integrating an existential lifestyle into your personal world? Marilyn is strongest in this area, even stronger than Jane—who may be the most authentic of the sample group. Marilyn's basic philosophic authenticity—undeveloped up to now—is further confirmed by her high time (T) score. A sense for the unity of time parallels an accurate perception of the structure of consciousness that is central to the field-of-consciousness theory of humankind. One is tempted to diagnose Marilyn as healthy and strong, but somewhat underdeveloped. Beth, on the other hand, seems to have difficulty with the notion of pure consciousness or the transcendental ego—which is the source of values and strengths. If true, this would weaken all other aspects of her personality. A good course in existential philosophy may be an excellent prescription for Beth.

6. Study other individual area scores. For example, what is your capacity to manage suffering? In our illustrations, only Mark and Jane have demonstrated that they possess this all-important quality. Beth, the youngest of the group, has the most trouble with that area of her personality.

7. Look for clues. The test can provide clues on how to work most efficiently toward a more authentic human existence. For example, Marilyn scores very low in the inwardness area of her profile; however, she scores surprisingly high on the reverence (Rv) item. It is of course quite possible that her Rv score reflects a purely intellectual rather than an experienced score, whereas her other scores in the inwardness area (SR, I, E) may be emotional and feeling in origin. Even so, that would be of little consequence in prescribing for her an individual program to achieve authenticity. She—or her friend, counselor, teacher, or therapist—must explore the role of the theme of reverence (for herself as well as for others) in her life. It is a strength on which she can build. If the capacity and willingness for reverence is one of her personality assets, she can use it as a clue to lift and build up her sagging self-confidence, independence, and self-respect.

Beth is also low in the inwardness area. She can raise her sense of inner strength, her maturity and feelings of personal solidity by exploring what is behind her relatively high individuality (I) score. She will find a living asset on which and with which she can build.

8. Watch for very high scores. As was suggested earlier, exceedingly high T scores must be approached cautiously. More likely than not they are an exaggeration and may indicate the exact opposite of what they appear to be on the surface. For example, look at the high score for D on Mark's profile. On the one hand, his high D score, together with the other high scores in the area of suffering, may be an index of strength and stoic acceptance of the negative realities of life. However, the exaggeratd score on D, when compared to a low degree of hope as indicated by a low Difference score, might have quite different and more dramatic meanings. To Mark, the virtue of death may be that it is the only hope in a totally hopeless life. Mark may be out-and-out suicidal. Death is then accepted as a beautiful way out of a life that has lost all meaning. This direction of questioning is worth pursuing in the case of Mark.

Individual Profiles

We are now ready for a closer look at our sample profiles.

Outstanding in Mark's profile is his survival power. Also, his low score on TS may be related to his physiologically-oriented medical outlook on life. He may be disinclined to make room for the concept of pure consciousness because the emphasis in medicine is on the body as the truly human part of ourselves. One consequence of a low TS score is, perhaps, his equally low Rv score. If there is no inward consciousness, then there is nothing to revere either. The high suffering and low Rv and Rs scores suggest an ethical but nonreligious man. Similarly, a high score on the Rs-E-Rv constellation—all of which are references to the realm of pure, extraworldly consciousness—would indicate, probably, a religious nature.

Beth is young. In a younger group she would have higher scores. Significant in Beth's profile is her relatively high Cm score. But her belief in her ability to make commitments—that is, her capacity to relate herself successfully to the world outside—is not borne out by her perception of time, growth, or love. But if she were to see the connections among these four themes, she might be able to use her apparent ability to make commitments for the sake of the other world-relating values. The thought that she is "ready to risk love" may be the right stimulus for growth in Beth. Her low time score, however, might indicate an improper perception of the continuity of consciousness. Time is a central category in existential thought. In fact, it is synonymous with the outward motion of the field of consciousness itself. Her low time score is confirmed, as it were, by her merely average FT score and her generally low ontology score. But because commitment is Beth's highest self-rating, any therapist or philosopher beginning to counsel with her on the basis of the self-assessment of the profile will do well to emphasize her self-perception of being able to make *individual* (I score) *commitments* (Cm score).

Significant in Marilyn's profile—in contrast to Beth's—is her very high time score, a sign that she is experiencing the world as a unified forward-moving continuity, realistically rooted in the here and now. Her time score is supported also by her high FT, TS, and G scores. That support makes her T score reliable. In any event, it is not common to exaggerate T. We also notice her very low SR, I, E, F, and Lv scores. We have already come across the thought that she is probably basically a very healthy person and can use that health to build up her authenticity. Inauthenticity in her case is learned and probably not very deep-seated. Her high SD item indicates an eager readiness to work with herself. One suspects that Marilyn is a strong and healthy person but still undeveloped. Her inauthenticity is superficial, but the roots of her authenticity seem to be deep indeed. She probably does not understand the full impact of her response to the ontological and methodological questions. But her self-evaluation does indicate, in existential terms, a thoroughly healthy and authentic manner of being-in-the-world. She *is* a field of consciousness, even though she may not understand the full implications of that concept.

Mahlon is also ready to work with himself, as indicated by a high SD score. That goal may be fatuous, however, because he seems spoiled and self-indulgent: he is not willing to accept responsibility for his life (Rs), cannot take pain (P), and seems to have said "no" to life (Li). His inability to reflect (Rf) contradicts his openness for SD. His Difference score is probably experienced as guilt, because of his low QII score. It may be possible to turn such an interpretation around and point out to him that his Difference score gives him a place to go in life, gives him meaning and the needed challenge for fulfillment. His extremely low freedom score (F), confirmed by an equally low responsibility score (Rs) is a bad omen. He is still a child; he is neither willing nor able to take charge of his life. As a result, his good adaptability score (A) is probably more a sign of spinelessness than strength of survival. But we must grasp every straw of strength—the probably hackneyed goals of

growth and self-disclosure. His strengths are not clearly defined. SD, G, and a little I are not enough to support him in
the march to authenticity.

Mahlon's profile is saltatory; it jumps all over the place. The
impression one gets is that his life is in turmoil, that nothing is
settled, and that he lacks the inner resources to deal with what
life has to offer at this time. The only area of consistency, and
it is partial at best, is found in his perception of his free will.
And what we see is not good; it is an indication of weakness, of
enslavement to fate — a theme underscored even more heavily
by his extremely low Rs score: He does not feel in control of his
life. Additional work in the areas of SD and G (which at least
intellectually exist in him) might begin to change the profile
dramatically and disclose his real strengths to him.

Another characteristic of Mahlon's profile is that suffering
and free will are relatively low, whereas encounter is relatively
high. His suffering score is disturbing, an indication he is
stopped in life by its negative aspects. He seems to follow the
growth movement's opinion that encounter leads to meaning.
However, the existential point of view is that the capacity to
integrate suffering into a total life and the ability to stand
alone are the genuine prerequisites for successful living.
Mahlon lacks these qualities at the present.

The situation with Beth is similar. She is average in "encounter" but weak in the integration of suffering. She can expect no progress in self-transcendence until she strengthens her
integration of suffering. One asset is that her free will score is
average at least.

Marilyn is strong in the encounter dimension, average in the
integration of life's negations, low in inner strength. One way
for Marilyn to make progress toward authenticity is to increase
the Difference score. She must be invited to adopt the existential goals of authenticity intellectually and conceptually. Because the difference is below average, her ambition for authenticity is modest and her perception of the goals that are
possible may be inadequate, especially vis-a-vis her healthy
potential. Her conceptual goals (answer to QI) can be raised

by additional formal education in the liberal arts. With it, her Difference score can be raised, and new movement can be brought into her life. A good guess is that the first effect of added education would be to raise her inwardness scores, which will then immediately be reflected in uniformly high scores in the encounter area.

Let us now examine some of the characteristics of Mark's profile. One notices first, perhaps, what is an unusual combination of a high Rf and A self-evaluation. In existential terms this means that Mark probably and correctly perceives himself as having high survival value: he is flexible and adaptable. He is flexible in locating his center between subjectivity and objectivity, and he is adaptable in that he can constitute and reconstitute his values and his lifestyle in accordance with his own decisions. Mark's survival potential is one of his great strengths. It is possible that he may be a troubled man, as was discussed earlier. His capacity for philosophical survival—which he probably does not understand conceptually but practices in actuality—has not only prevented his collapse over these years but also given him an outwardly successful life (M.D., five children, etc.).

A negative feature of Mark's profile is that the bulk of his low scores are in the encounter and self-transcendence area. That G is high while Cm, Lv, and T are low is a possible indication of where his clue for added strength lies. He seems willing to grow, and the growth that he needs lies in the encounter, in the meeting—of the world and the Other—aspect of human existence.

A strong inwardness score should make strong encounters possible. But Mark's low Rv score is in the way. And what holds back his reverence for subjectivity is his resistance to self-disclosure (SD) as well as his (professionally based?) rejection of the idea of a consciousness that is not the same as the body (indicated by a low TS rating). The high E rating, which is amazingly out of character with a low TS score, is a highly significant ray of hope.

The constellation of low scores consists of TS, SD, Rv, Cm,

and Lv. These are related categories. They must all be raised for authenticity. Mark has the strength to do it, as indicated by his competence in integrating suffering into his life (the most outstanding single area score) and his rather high score in the inwardness area. Mark evidently perceives himself as having considerable inner strength.

Another surprising contradiction is the high G score and the low SD score. These must be brought together to make the process toward authenticity a realistic one. The SD score is likely to be more accurate than the G score. It is possible to give an intellectual and thus meaningless response to item C13 (G). Item B (SD) elicits more of an experiential response. The contradiction may indicate self-deception.

Mark should start working with whatever theme or area of strength suits him best. It will not take long to discover where that is. He must increase the difference between his concept of life and his actual life, his ideal and his reality (QI and QII). That will give him hope. As with Marilyn, it can probably be accomplished, at least in part, through the academic study of a philosophy of humankind. He has the willpower and self-discipline necessary to achieve philosophic growth, as his free will area indicates.

Mark's profile is his perception of himself; it is a projection, which exaggerates certain features, of how it feels to be him. He is now in a good position to take a fresh look at himself as he himself has projected himself.

Question I

We notice immediately that Scott's score for QI is considerably higher than his score in QII. That is not necessarily to be expected, because we are dealing with statistical averages and not absolute figures. The discrepancy seems to be healthy, in that it gives him meanings toward which to strive. The slopes of the two curves are also similar, with perhaps one interesting exception—there is a crossover, or at least a meeting of lines, in the free will area. He is saying to himself that his acceptance (F, QI) and use (Li, QI) of freedom, in connection with what he actually lives (F, QII and Li, QII) leaves less room for hope, growth, and progress than is the case in any other area of his life. He is stuck in life, his high hopes to the contrary notwithstanding, because he possesses a limited conception of his freedom. That may be the most significant aspect of this profile, a fact borne out by my personal knowledge of the individual. Scott is a bright student, well-informed in existential matters. Nevertheless, he feels paralyzed; he cannot realize what he thinks are his meanings. His profile gives us a clue: ignorance of freedom. Counseling bore out the contention that he did not really understand the enormous possibilities of his human freedom.

Our next focus will be the areas of greatest difference between QI and QII scores. These are to be found in the FT, Rs, Cd, SR, I, T, and A scales. The biggest gap is on the I scale. The following descriptive speculations are worth considering. It is his perception (which is far above the average, because on the average the answers to Questions I and II would coincide on the profile) that his sense of being an individual is far less than what it should be. In truth, Scott was a very timid, self-effacing, insecure, and ineffective person. This diagnosis is corroborated by his other high differential scores.

The FT separation shows that, whereas conceptually he feels the obligation to experience ego and world as unitary, he does not feel that this is in any way the case. We have here an alienated individual who believes himself to be cut off from the world. The Rs separation would appear to indicate a puerile, immature avoidance of responsibility for his own life. It suggests a dependent and passive personality. The A gap implies a similar spoiled and self-indulgent childish personality structure. These points of immaturity are further supported by the large SR gap.

What suggestions for therapeutic strategy emerge from this profile? His actual strength (as perceived by him) is P, with possibly the addition of SD, Li, and Rf. A high P would indicate a tragic sense of life, which could either mean inauthentic self-pity or authentic capacity for tolerating and integrating the negativities of life. The latter would be a most commendable strength, one on which a therapist can build. A high score on both SD and Rf would indicate a capacity for therapeutic growth. He probably would be a competent and cooperative patient. A high Li score would indicate that he is motivated to grow in therapy.

These strengths are, in general, corroborated by his scores on QI. Further, the high Rs and E scores on QI are worth noting. They indicate the conviction, at least, that the job of growing to authenticity through self-disclosure is fully his responsibility. They also suggest that he is prepared to understand the strength and security that can be derived from an understanding of the nature of our human consciousness, as indicated in items C6 and C6a on the Master Table.

If my suggestions for interpretation in this chapter have proven to be inadequate, I suggest that when you are ready to examine your own profile you use your creative imagination and allow your intuition to roam freely. Your personal profile can be highly suggestive in understanding yourself in terms of the categories and themes of existential philosophy.

AUTHENTICITY PROFILE

Name: _____   T-Score 80

Summary		
1197	1211	399

Band	Summary	QI/QII	Ontology (FT TS Rs / A1 A2 A3)	(SD / B)	Suffering (P D Cd / C1 C2 C14)	Inwardness (SR I E Rv / C4 C5 C6 C6a)	Free will (F LI / C7 C8)	Encounter and self-transcendence (CM Lv T G / C9 C10 C12 C13)	Survival (RI A / C3 C11)	T-Score
Far Above Average	1152 1064 297	QI	(69) (76) (71)		(68) (70) (66)	(70) (73) (75) (77)		(71) (72) (72)		
		QII	(61) (68) (64)	(69)	(63) (63) (61)	(63) (65) (65) (69)	(68) (65)	(66) (67) (69) (70)	(64) (70)	70
Above Average	1107 917 194	QI	50 60 58	(61)	57 55 53	55 60 54 60	(61) (61)	57 60 59 (63)	(64) (61)	
		QII	50 54 54	57	51 49 48	50 53 47 54	55 53	53 55 56 59	54 58	60
Average	862 770 92	QI	43 45 44	51	45 41 40	40 47 34 44	47 48	44 49 47 53	49 51	
		QII	39 40 43	45	39 36 35	37 42 29 38	43 42	39 42 43 49	45 46	50
Below Average	717 623 -10	QI	30 30 30	40	34 26 27	35 34 14 28	34 35	31 37 35 43	34 40	
		QII	28 25 32	39	27 22 22	24 30 10 22	30 30	26 29 30 38	32 34	40
Far Below Average	572 476 -118	QI	17 15 17	30	22 11 14	21 21 (-7) 11	21 22	18 26 13 33	20 29	
		QII	16 11 21	22	16 8 9	2 19 (-8) 6	17 18	13 16 17 28	21 23	30
	427 329 -215	QI	4 10 3	19	11 (-6) 1	6 8 (-5)	8 10	5 14 1 23	5 19	
	QI QII Diff	QII	5 7 10	11	4 (-6) (-4)	(-11) 7 (-10)	4 7	(-1) 3 4 17	1 11	20

(I-II)

FT TS Rs	SD	P D Cd	SR I E Rv	F LI	CM Lv T G	RI A
A1 A2 A3	B	C1 C2 C14	C4 C5 C6 C6a	C7 C8	C9 C10 C12 C13	C3 C11
Ontology	Meth-odology	Suffering	Inwardness	Free will	Encounter and self-transcendence	Survival
WORLD VIEW		PHILOSOPHICAL ANTHROPOLOGY				

QI ___
QII ___

Sex: _____ Children _____
Age: _____
Marital Status: _____
Occupation: _____

AUTHENTICITY PROFILE

Name: _____   T-Score 80

Summary		
1197	1211	399

Band	Summary	QI/QII	Ontology (FT TS Rs / A1 A2 A3)	(SD / B)	Suffering (P D Cd / C1 C2 C14)	Inwardness (SR I E Rv / C4 C5 C6 C6a)	Free will (F LI / C7 C8)	Encounter and self-transcendence (CM Lv T G / C9 C10 C12 C13)	Survival (RI A / C3 C11)	T-Score
Far Above Average	1152 1064 297	QI	(69) (76) (71)		(68) (70) (66)	(70) (73) (75) (77)		(71) (72) (72)		
		QII	(61) (68) (64)	(69)	(63) (63) (61)	(63) (65) (65) (69)	(68) (65)	(66) (67) (69) (70)	(64) (70)	70
Above Average	1107 917 194	QI	50 60 58	(61)	57 55 53	55 60 54 60	(61) (61)	57 60 59 (63)	(64) (61)	
		QII	50 54 54	57	51 49 48	50 53 47 54	55 53	53 55 56 59	54 58	60
Average	862 770 92	QI	43 45 44	51	45 41 40	40 47 34 44	47 48	44 49 47 53	49 51	
		QII	39 40 43	45	39 36 35	37 42 29 38	43 42	39 42 43 49	45 46	50
Below Average	717 623 -10	QI	30 30 30	40	34 26 27	35 34 14 28	34 35	31 37 35 43	34 40	
		QII	28 25 32	39	27 22 22	24 30 10 22	30 30	26 29 30 38	32 34	40
Far Below Average	572 476 -118	QI	17 15 17	30	22 11 14	21 21 (-7) 11	21 22	18 26 13 33	20 29	
		QII	16 11 21	22	16 8 9	2 19 (-8) 6	17 18	13 16 17 28	21 23	30
	427 329 -215	QI	4 10 3	19	11 (-6) 1	6 8 (-5)	8 10	5 14 1 23	5 19	
	QI QII Diff	QII	5 7 10	11	4 (-6) (-4)	(-11) 7 (-10)	4 7	(-1) 3 4 17	1 11	20

(I-II)

FT TS Rs	SD	P D Cd	SR I E Rv	F LI	CM Lv T G	RI A
A1 A2 A3	B	C1 C2 C14	C4 C5 C6 C6a	C7 C8	C9 C10 C12 C13	C3 C11
Ontology	Meth-odology	Suffering	Inwardness	Free will	Encounter and self-transcendence	Survival
WORLD VIEW		PHILOSOPHICAL ANTHROPOLOGY				

QI ___
QII ___

Sex: _____ Children _____
Age: _____
Marital Status: _____
Occupation: _____

58

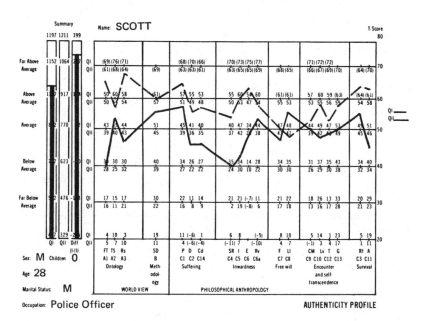

5
Diana

Diana could be very attractive, but is at present very much overweight. She seems to know instinctively that philosophy will assist her in understanding her many problems and helpfully support her in resolving her tragic agony. Understandably her problems are deeply disturbing to her and in this letter she has not much hope.

Dear Dr. Koestenbaum:

First of all I must say that I am afraid that you might make fun of what I have to say. If the following is inane or irrelevant to this course, please pass it by. I am afraid of you. Your existence, like a blinding light, diminishes my existence into darkness because I am not quite real yet.

Now to get to the subject of my concern. I would like to discuss guilt. You say that guilt is good because it means that you have made a decision but what if that guilt paralyzes your life? Perhaps the presence of guilt means that you have not accepted the responsibility for your decision.

I have two major guilts that have in fact paralyzed my life and closed me up inside myself afraid to take from life (people) or give to life (people). One of these guilts is connected with my child who was born out of wedlock. She is now four years old and I now regret that I did not give her up for adoption by a woman and a man who could give her the things I cannot. I feel inadequate as a mother but am unwilling to give her up now because she is part of me—I am part of her—she is a reminder of my sexuality, my fertility, and selfishly I am unwilling to give that reminder up. This is my decision but my guilt burrows into my heart like a tick and I cannot breathe.

My second guilt is my feeling of responsibility for my father's death. He walked in on my boyfriend and me when we were in bed making love. He blew up, raged then escaped to the obscurity of alcohol for three days, after which he returned home and consumed a bottle of sleeping pills. I have for these past two years felt responsible for his suicide. This has paralyzed my personal life. I have been unable to have a meaningful relationship with another human being since then. I want to give but feel incapable of it.

These two guilts have led me to depths of despair out of which I have not yet been able to rise. My life is meaningless. My existence is less than a single tear drop in the vastness of humanity's existence. No one needs me in this world. I am essential to no one. I am cold, afraid and alone. But what frightens me more than my own loneliness is the realization that we are *all* lonely sad creatures pathetically reaching out for contact. Perhaps it is the search that provides meaning for existence and not the attainment of the goal. If this is so then we must all keep reaching.

Diana

Before I can help Diana with her problems, I must help her understand the letter she wrote. Thus, before she analyzes the *content* of her letter she must be helped to examine its *form*. Diana's problems disturb her so much that she alternately quivers and is paralyzed as she attempts to discuss them privately with me. Her whole being is deeply *involved* with her guilts, her inadequacies, and her despair with her late father, her daughter, and her own overweight body. She is so *close* to her suffering that she *is* her suffering. Diana must be encouraged, even urged, to step out of the deep involvement with her body and her problems and look at her whole life situation with ascetic detachment. She must disengage her mind from her anxiety so that she can reflect on it and discuss it. I invited her to read her letter to me out loud.

I urged her not only to hear her voice but also to think of the letter as coming from someone else. In existential philosophy I call this first step in self-understanding *reflection* rather than *being*. I have here invoked the principle of reflection from the Master Table ("I am able both to *live* my life and to *reflect* on my life"). As she reads her statement and thinks of it as coming from another person, she *reflects* on herself and her letter rather than merely *being* herself and her life. She is now no longer the Diana in the letter but also the *detached observer of the Diana in the letter.*

This deceptively simple act of reflection has nevertheless the potential for marvelous strength-giving and even therapeutic powers. You can do the same by talking *about* your problem rather than by *having* or *living* your problem.

Even before she goes into any details of her problem — that is, before she analyzes the content of her letter — she has, by listening to herself, made several important discoveries with wide application.

Reflection leads her now to her first big insight: There is always hope. By *reflecting* on her life instead of *being* her life she has discovered hope. She sees her life in perspective; she can fit it into the larger world of which she is a part. Inevitably, the problem is thereby diminished. She now says, "I can think of worse things!" "I am thankful I have a lovely daughter!" "How beautiful it is that I am still living and not dead like my father!" The beauties of nature now become sacred gifts to her. Perspective always gives hope. She discovers that there are no truly hopeless situations. She learns that the secret of finding the hopeful ingredient in any situation, no matter how desperate, is to see it in perspective.

By merely reflecting on her behavior, she has made a discovery that is of the deepest concern to all human beings of all nations in all of history: the need for and the reality of hope.

Hope is the knowledge that I am time, that the consciousness and the ego that I *am* is in truth the forward movement in time. Hope means that the future is real and is mine. Hopelessness, on the other hand, is the illusion that I am *not* time, that time does not exist. Diana has discovered the truth of the principles of time and of growth ("I experience time as living in a present which, while utilizing the past, connects directly and primarily into my future," and "My life is an endless process of growing, emerging, and reaching out"). The more she integrates that truth into her daily life, the healthier she will be.

Reflection now leads Diana to a second major discovery: She

has already *acted* to help herself. She has not only written about her suffering, but she has also done much more. The action of writing down her problem in itself gave her some perspective and distance. But beyond that, *she acted in submitting the problem to me and having it discussed.* Reflecting on her letter, she discovers it as more than a letter: It is an *action* that has enabled her to put herself in touch with the very world from which she had been alienated! Diana's writing is already part of Diana's solution. She has now discovered that she can make a commitment and thereby has already overcome, in part, her deep alienation. She has discovered the principle of *commitment* from the Master Table. She has established identification and contact with the world of people that heretofore seemed inaccessible to her. In a manner of speaking, she has already achieved the goal she seeks: communication, contact, being extroverted in the world rather than introverted in an alienated self.

The discovery that she can act—indeed, that she *has* acted—*is also the discovery that her alienation from the world has already begun to be overcome.* To have acted, rather than merely to have thought, is to have overcome the gap between self and world that characterizes mental illness. To have acted is to have built a firm bridge between the formerly isolated, depressed, and ineffectual self and the real and permanent world beyond. When Diana recognizes that she, an insular ego, has made a commitment to the world around her by the simple expedient of submitting her letter and reading it out loud, she is able to understand the essential nature of human existence, as expressed in the field theory of humankind ("I am neither a body nor a soul but a continuous consciousness-body-world field").

A small rock jutting above the waves of the ocean has now been recognized by her to be but the peak of an enormous underwater mountain. The small rock is her small act of submitting a letter for discussion. The vast mountain that it reveals is the truth about people, the field-of-consciousness theory of humankind. Diana now discovers that the vast underwater mountain has other peaks that show above the surface many miles from the first. To Diana this insight means she can act in other areas of her life as well. She can act not only by submitting a letter but also by raising her daughter, establishing new and healthy relations with men, and making meaningful contact with the academic environment in which she is living.

Furthermore, the principle of reflection leads Diana to a third discovery, one that is as important as it is difficult to understand. In reflecting on her problem—as opposed to being steeped in it—Diana has discovered her true philosophic center; she has uncovered the roots of her genuine support and her true foundation. She has discovered her pure consciousness, her untarnished awareness. She is now in the presence of an insight as ancient and as venerable as humankind itself. She recognizes that her true nature, her true self, is not her paralysis, her guilt about her father, her inadequacy as a mother, or even her overweight body. On the contrary, her true self and nature—the authentic Diana—is *the distance from* her insufferable world; and this distance is *created by the act of reflection itself.* The magic power of reflection is ancient wisdom in the history of humankind (Eastern mystics and Western ascetics) and it is also a recent discovery in psychotherapy (the power of talking *about* our problems). Great revolutions are based on simple ideas.

A swimmer in the water is at one with the water. A swimmer outside the water, looking at it from a distance, knows that in truth he is different from the water. Diana has discovered for herself the truth and the importance of the principle of eternity from the Master Table ("There exists a consciousness within me which I am and which is eternal").

Civilization has called the psychological distance manifested by the magic act of reflection on one's troubles the *self* or *consciousness, spirit* or *awareness,* even *ego, subjectivity,* and *inwardness,* and sometimes the *soul.* The fact remains that the principle of reflection shows to us our genuine center, the awareness or consciousness that we in reality are. All health, all joy and happiness begins in that spiritual center. All of

Diana's strength, power, and independence, all control over her life and over her destiny, all these have their roots in her spiritual or conscious center. And Diana made the discovery of the nature of her consciousness by the simple act of reading her letter as if it were someone else's. She learned to *look at* herself rather than to *be* herself.

What this means is that she is now already in touch with the source of all her strength and with the foundation of her security. She has tapped her inner reservoir of power, which can give her meaning by overcoming her alienation.

You see a movie that touches you deeply, and the tears stream down your cheeks. You and the movie are one. What happens on the screen happens to you. But that is your false self: In reality you are of course not on the screen. Suddenly you realize that your weeping is seen by someone whose observation of your emotion embarrasses you. Instantly your oneness with the movie situation disappears and your center, your true self, is experienced to be at a distance from the screen. You console yourself by saying, "It is just a movie; I am different from the movie." It is that distance which discloses to you the pure consciousness that is you. That is the meaning of reflection.

The same access to your inward center is made possible if the movie scares you. While you are in the state of being terrified, you are one with the movie. You can forcibly disengage yourself from this total identification by realizing that you are only observing a movie and are not immersed in it. Once you succeed, you have achieved the sense of control and peace that comes with the distance of reflection. As you are scared by the movie, you say to yourself "It's only a movie; it is not reality." In this way, you move from illusion (identity with the movie) to reality (distance from the movie). And now remember that you are the distance between the screen and your ego; that distance is your true self.

Diana has come home.

Finally *Diana has discovered the nature of her true self—* that is, the pure consciousness that is her being. She has understood experientially the truth of the fact that her inner self is her home and her dignity, which is the principle of reverence ("Each individual human inward subjectivity is the divine consciousness in that person"). She has also understood that she is in reality two selves ("I am a pure consciousness that has a psychological personality, a physical body, and many roles"). She is Diana the observer of her problems and Diana the problem itself. To clarify this point is somewhat more difficult than to explain Diana's other discoveries.

The completed act of reflection discloses to Diana the fundamental philosophical fact that a human being is an independent consciousness *in addition* to being a person, a body, and a series of social roles. While Diana is *reflecting* on her performance—as she does when we discuss it—she is not the Diana who *has* the problems, nor is she the Diana who "looks at," "knows," "understands," "sees," and "perceives" the Diana with the problems. There are two Dianas in existence here. One is the empirical Diana, the Diana with problems, anxieties, and depression. The other is the transcendental Diana— Diana the observer. Diana the observer is pure consciousness, pure self, pure ego. That Diana *is not* a problem, *does not have* a problem, but is a neutral observer *looking at* the Diana with problems.

She is now in a position to acquire the sense of security and rootedness that comes from recognizing her true self as inward consciousness, and this is the principle of self-reliance ("I am an adult consciousness that exists alone: I choose to be independent and self-reliant"). In that consciousness lie all her strengths and her answers.

Diana has accomplished significant existential achievements through the extremely simple device of reflection. The principle of reflection states, "I am able both to *live* my life and to *reflect* on my life." She reflected on her problem by writing it down, by reading her letter out loud and pretending it was written by another, and by sharing the letter with someone she trusted. As a consequence, Diana has already achieved several insightful and therapeutic experiences. She had discovered that there is real hope for her; that she can act—that is, that she has already overcome her alienation from the world; and she has discovered her true conscious self—the free spirit or consciousness that she is—and that this consciousness is her home, where she has her roots. These discoveries have universal validity; they are the philosophical truths about human beings in general. In short, she can say to herself:

1. I am respected.
2. I have hope.
3. I can act to improve my life.
4. I am in touch with the world (I have overcome alienation).
5. I am in touch with my center.
6. I am strong.
7. I have found my home.

In order for us to help Diana we must point out her strengths. She has many, and they are real. She ends her letter with a profound insight:

But what frightens me more than my own loneliness is the realization that we are all lonely sad creatures pathetically reaching out for contact. Perhaps it is the search that provides meaning for existence and not the attainment of the goal. If this is so then we must all keep reaching.

She is here telling us not what frightens her most, but rather the source of her hope. This is one unmistakable evidence of her strength.

She announces, first of all, that she will solve the problem herself. "Perhaps it is the search that provides meaning for existence and not the attainment of the goal. If this is so then we must all keep reaching." She does not expect others to solve her problems for her because she already possesses the strength to say *yes* to life and to reconstruct it into happier habits. That strength is a sign of great health. She may have a more difficult life than that experienced by other young women; however, she fully measures up to the occasion by *telling us* that she will solve her own problems. What a privilege for us to be permitted to witness such a beautiful expression of strength, life affirmation, and courage under these painful circumstances!

Diana, in the second place, has used the principle of life ("My first and last choice is to say *yes* to life"). To say *yes* to life is not an automatic act: It is a *choice* that all of us can make. And Diana has made that choice. Had she ended her letter in despair or with threats of suicide, her choice would have been to say *no* to life. She says *yes* in her determination to succeed, in her will to be happy, and in her choosing hope over despair.

We all possess that power. It is the power of freedom and it is expressed in theme C7 ("I always choose because I am always free"). Some of us use our freedom to choose despair and to give up, whereas others choose to fight, win, and conquer.

Third, Diana demonstrates deep philosophical wisdom—that is, insight into an eternal truth—when she writes, "We are *all* lonely sad creatures pathetically reaching out for contact . . . We must all keep reaching." She had discovered the universal human truth of the principle of self-reliance ("I am an adult consciousness that exists alone: I choose to be independent and self-reliant"). She has thereby discovered that human beings are a brotherhood of aliens and a commune of strangers. She has uncovered the ancient wisdom that although each of us is totally alone in this world we nevertheless can lovingly share that tragedy with others.

As a result, she knows, fourth, the meaning of love, kindness, compassion, and intimacy as expressed in principle C10 ("As an adult I can choose to meet, confront, witness, understand, and be mirrored by another; I can also choose to love and care for that person"), even though she has not yet been able to integrate it meaningfully into her actual life. Diana may be totally alone, but she also knows that everyone else is likewise totally alone. And thus she understands that in the pathos of suffering, human beings get close, meet each other, love and respect each other, and achieve a sense of genuine in-

timacy. The beauty of being accepted and of accepting another human being unconditionally—that is, the beauty of
both loving and being loved—is possible only on a foundation
of aloneness and a sharing of suffering.

Fifth, Diana has a feeling for the tragic sense of life, which
leads her to insights into the principles of pain and death ("I
choose to value my pains" and "I choose to value my limitations"). Only by understanding how painfully alone she is and
how all others are equally painfully alone can she understand
the meaning of the existential way of life. We thus can point
out to Diana her real strengths, strengths whose existence is an
inspiration to all those who have the good sense to perceive
them. Her basic health rests on the fact that her letter of
alienation nevertheless discloses real understanding of the
principles of the Master Table, and with it of the existential
way of life.

We learn from Diana's strengths the following:

1. When in despair, recognize and list your strengths.
2. You have the power to say *yes* to life. Use it!
3. If you feel alone, remember that we are all alone.
4. You can overcome loneliness by *sharing* loneliness. If you
   are able to reflect on yourself—get out of yourself—then
   you are also worthy and capable of love.
5. If you understand the tragic sense of life you have the potential for maturity and authenticity.

6

Diana's Guilt

Not all guilt experiences are the same: Some are bad, unhealthy, and destructive. They paralyze action, stunt growth, and may even lead to the deep depressions that end in suicide. Other guilt experiences are constructive and healthy. "Bad guilt," which the existentialist calls neurotic or pathological guilt, can be cured. "Good guilt," so-called existential guilt, cannot be cured. This latter guilt is in the essence of humanity. These guilt experiences are natural and inevitable. To remove or "cure" existential guilt is like curing high blood pressure by draining the blood, or curing shortness of breath by surgically removing the lungs.

Guilt is, for Diana, a pervasive state of mind. To deal with her guilt and the lifestyle produced by it, she must first confront her experiences and feelings of guilt. She must get into her guilt, feel it fully and in detail rather than trying to escape it. She must not fear her guilt feelings but have the courage to open herself to them. That activity in itself involves an understanding of the rule for self-disclosure ("I must be fully disclosed to myself both as a human being and as *Diana*) as well as of the principles of death and limits from the Master Table. The guilty person can gain strength, maturity, and joy as the result of a direct confrontation with that kind of guilt.

"Bad" guilt is neurotic; "good" guilt is existential. And Diana has both kinds of guilt. In helping Diana, we must show her that her guilts about her illicit affair, her father's death, her illegitimate daughter, her incompetence as a mother, and her failure as a friend and lover all contain in them a grain of wisdom, a portion of universal truth about the human condition. She is in error if she thinks of her guilt as all bad. Her guilt can reveal to Diana the universal truth of the human condition. It can lead to insight. Guilt is a means to self-disclosure, and the wisdom thus gained can make one free.

In general, suffering and pain can be for Diana—as they have been for many human beings—the foundation of what is deep and meaningful in life. Suffering and pain can push open the doors to health-giving philosophical knowledge about humanity and the world. Rather than thinking of Diana's guilt merely as an illness, we must recognize that it is rich in creative truths about man's eternal essence. In other words, there is a cosmic dimension to Diana's suffering. She is sitting on a treasure and does not know it.

If Diana feels guilty, it is not because she violated a rule: She feels guilty because she *is* guilty, and she *is* guilty because she has exercised her freedom. She recognizes this in her letter, but only conceptually, not experientially. Guilt is a pain to be valued and not a feeling to be repressed or tranquilized. *Guilt is proof that one has used and is now using one's freedom.* In short, guilt is proof of one's authenticity. Only computers feel no guilt. The person who has no sense of guilt should worry. He or she has no surface evidence of being free—no evidence of decision-making, no evidence of the intuition that he or she could have chosen differently and independently, no evidence of responsibility for self-determined actions.

What distinguishes Diana—and all of us—from animals? The fact that she is free, the fact that she makes choices and decisions, that she can create an identity for herself and for her child, that she can choose to do and she can also choose not to do. Her freedom makes Diana human. In fact, it is her freedom that makes Diana, and the rest of us godlike. To choose means to say *yes* to one thing by saying *no* to another. Diana chose a sexual affair rather than a nonsexual life. In saying *yes* to sex she said *no* to celibacy. The sense of joy resulted from yes-saying, whereas the sense of guilt derives from no-saying: To the extent she said *no* to the rules of premarital celibacy she felt guilt. Joy is proof of a decision made, but so is

guilt. Her guilt is but the realization that she made a decision.
And decision-making is an authentic, free, and human activity.

The practical consequence of knowing about existential
guilt is a new mindset. Before philosophy, Diana insistently
demanded (unconsciously) that she get rid of her guilt. She felt
defective because of her guilt (she felt guilty about her guilt).
Now, after philosophy, she feels *adequate* because of her guilt.
She has learned to live with it. She has learned to feel comfortable and real *because* she feels guilt, resting peacefully, as it
were, supported by the couch that is her guilt.

If Diana's actions had been reversed and she had abstained
from sex with her boyfriend, the basic joy-guilt pattern would
have remained unchanged. Then her joy would have been
based on consistency with her father's principles and the rules
of society; her joy would then have been in the affirmation of
"character" and "obedience." Because she violated these rules
by sleeping with her boyfriend, she is guilty. The options were
society and father against boyfriend and sex. She chose the latter. Knowing she could have used her freedom to choose the
former makes her feel guilty.

Nothing would have changed if she had chosen otherwise.
Let us assume she used her freedom to choose society and
father rather than boyfriend and sex. Her guilt would not be
that of unfulfilled possibilities; this would have been a free
decision against expressing her feminine sexuality. Again she
would have made a choice: duty over guilt. Seeing that guilt is
inevitable transforms Diana's perception of the meaning of
guilt from something sick and destructive to something
human, healthy, and elevating. In her very guilt can be the
seeds of her happiness.

We learn from these analyses that the joy-guilt, yes-no oscillation is the essence of life itself. It is not true that Diana would
be without guilt if she had lived differently. To be alive, to be
conscious, and to be a self or an ego, to exist in this world, is to
be in a state of stress. Polarization is natural. Diana has recognized the truth of the principle of contradiction: "The inescapable ambiguities and contradictions of life are my powerful
allies." Life is like a magnet—without the stress between the

positive and the negative poles there can exist no magnetic field in the first place. Consciousness itself is in its essence like a magnetic field. These are messages of hope rather than despair, of health and maturity rather than of sickness and inadequacy. Philosophy has helped Diana turn weakness into strength and despair into hope.

How can you learn from Diana's guilt? When you feel oppressed with guilt, remember the following:

1. Guilt is proof of freedom.
2. All life is conflict.
3. Your agony is normal rather than sick, existential rather than neurotic.
4. The existence of your guilt proves that you have
   a. the strength to *make decisions;*
   b. the strength to *evaluate* your own life by your own standards;
   c. the strength to *choose* and *maintain* your own standards and values.

We will examine each one of Diana's guilts separately to see what they teach us. She has four: (1) guilt about sex with her boyfriend, (2) guilt about her father's death, (3) guilt about her inadequacy as a mother, and (4) guilt about her inadequacy as a human being.

We have already discussed the first of these and derived the insight that her philosophical experiences will be essentially unchanged whichever way she chooses. She thus gains the courage to make her own decisions and establish her own evaluations.

Let us now consider Diana's guilt about her father. Her father's death is not a complicated matter, though it may seem so. From an objective point of view it is clear that Diana is not responsible for her father's death. Instead, she has *chosen* to hold herself responsible; she *wants* to be responsible for his death. One traditional psychological approach to Diana's guilt might run as follows: "You are not responsible for your father's death. You can get rid of your guilt feelings by seeing

the situation objectively. Psychotherapy can help you rid yourself of that guilt, which is merely the introjection of external
rules." An existential approach tells Diana: "Your guilt feelings are valid. You can be helped to perceive them as healthy
and strong rather than as sick and weak."

In this context, she must remember the principles of both
freedom and responsibility. In other words, Diana must
assume subjective responsibility for the death of her father,
but this is a responsibility over which she exercises full control,
which she adopts freely and rationally. It is not a responsibility
which controls her as if she were a marionette, because it is not
externally imposed. Although she is not responsible objectively, she must make his death hers, subjectively. In truth, she
already *has* made his death hers—she already *has* assumed responsibility for it, hence her painful feelings.

The situation is similar to the responsibility for a dream.
Objectively speaking, I am not responsible for the content of
my dreams. If I seek authenticity, however, I must choose to
assume responsibility for all aspects of my dreams. Then I am
ready to learn from them and use them therapeutically.

Diana is not responsible for her father's death in any objective, moral, or legal sense. Nevertheless, she must take full existential responsibility for his death if she wishes to gain control over her life. This decision is tricky business, but it is a
crucial one.

Underlying Diana's guilt feelings about her father's death
are the natural human resentments, violent feelings, and even
hate and wishes for the death of one's parents. These are normal feelings, and understanding them can be constructive in
plumbing one's own depths. Diana's disturbing death wishes
toward her father represented a choice. But her decision, far
deeper than ordinary memory or psychotherapy can take her,
to hate her father and wish him dead, is not necessarily an evil
one, for it does not kill. In fact, a person who has a clear perception of this fantasy wish and recognizes it as normal can as
a result have an excellent real relationship with her parent. It
is the person who hides this wish deeply in her consciousness

who is likely to have neurotic interchanges with her parents. Diana feels guilty because she did not love her father as she feels she should have; on the contrary, she hated him and wished him symbolically dead. And, true enough, her father answered her wish by actually dying. Her guilt is thus about an act or choice — the wish to have him dead. But even that wish is independent of any action her father might have taken.

The *philosophical* meaning of Diana's guilt is this: She chose her father's death. She is as responsible as if she had actually killed him. That, however, is the language of her inward consciousness, not that of the moral or the legal system.

But why is Diana's responsibility for the death wish of her father existentially important? *That Diana chooses to wish her father dead means that she affirms her own independence and difference.* By wishing him dead she is asserting her uniqueness; she announces that she is different from her father, that she is an individual. She says *yes* to herself through the device of saying *no* to the world. The underground shoots from the old tree have given rise elsewhere to a new tree. The connecting shoots can now rot or be cut; they are no longer needed. In fact, they interfere with the independent development of each separate tree. Diana has now discovered that *her guilt about her dead father is really the choice of her own independence.* She has discovered the meaning of the principles of self-reliance and individuality and she has used them ("I am an adult consciousness that exists alone: I choose to be independent and self-reliant," and "It is right and normal for me to seem different from other human beings").

Diana misunderstood her guilt feelings. She misunderstood the meaning of the secret death wish for her father: It was not a psychotic wish for his death but a healthy demand for her independence. The unfortunate circumstance of his actual death confused her decision. Philosophy can help her sort out her thoughts. Before philosophy she felt sick and paralyzed over her decision to kill the father within her. After philosophy she feels healthy and mobile over that decision.

The symbols of independence — which for her include the

sin of symbolic patricide—do not kill; on the contrary, they can help create a superbly mature relationship between the living daughter and her real father. It is the repression of the symbols for independence that can kill by eliminating the distance between subject and object. That distance in each of us guarantees rational knowledge and emotional control. The elimination of that distance creates a dangerous psychopathology.

It must be made clear to Diana that in analyzing the guilt about her father's death she has in fact made a fundamental philosophical discovery about human nature. The death wish toward a parent and its ensuing guilt are not proof of illness but the expression that there exists at the center of consciousness an authentic choice of self-affirmation, independence, and self-reliance. The philosophic insight into the revealing nature of that guilt leads Diana from an immature and neurotic perception of the daughter-father relationship to a mature and authentic person-to-person perception.

Gradually, Diana is recognizing the innate health, maturity, normalcy, and strength that naturally reside in her soul. As a result, she is now less likely than before to deprecate herself. Moreover, she has gained immense self-confidence merely by recognizing herself in a true philosophic light. No external facts have changed in Diana's life by virtue of this existential analysis of her consciousness. What has changed dramatically is her perception of her life. Its interpretation and meaning have been transformed. What before was sickness is now seen to contain a significant core of health. In fact, what appears to be sickness may in actual fact be an essential ingredient in health. What earlier was weakness is now seen to hide strength. And what once was ugliness and worthlessness is now recognized to contain beauty and dignity. Philosophic self-knowledge has accomplished that conversion for Diana.

How can one manage guilt? Socrates said "Know thyself." The goal of the philosophical life is self-disclosure—that is, an understanding as complete as possible of oneself and of how one is situated in the world. Diana must therefore understand what is behind her guilt about her father's death.

The case of Harry illustrates how this may be done. At 39, Harry is a successful research biochemist. When he was only seven, he witnessed his father's being bludgeoned to death by a robber who had broken into the family's house. As part of the therapy to help him discover deeper layers of meaning and insight behind that experience, Harry was submerged in a warm whirlpool bath, then rocked until he could recall and relive those early terrifying memories. What he recalled went far beyond ordinary memory, all the way to the philosophic foundations of human existence. At first he recalled his fright and despair at the loss. Then Harry began to discover the horrible truth that at one level of his being he had actually wanted and needed his father dead; thus the memory of the murder was worse than he expected because it was a wish come true. But why did Harry *want* his father dead? He *had* loved his father! Was Freud right, and was it true that little Harry was jealous of the relationship between his father and mother? Perhaps the Oedipal situation did exist and perhaps it does account for his death wish. Harry had been willing to accept that psychoanalytic interpretation but it did not remove his symptoms. His life was still meaningless. In being led back to even greater spiritual depths, Harry discovered that the secret death wish for his father was not only a matter of early childhood but remained with him throughout his entire life. What did that mean?

Harry did not want his real father dead—the flesh-and-blood person, the human being with inalienable rights to life, liberty, and the pursuit of happiness. He wanted that father dead whom he had swallowed into his own being, his personal center. And that father has to die for all of us. Harry needed to affirm his independence, his uniqueness, his *difference* from and lack of dependence on the world. His human essence is to demonstrate that he is not someone else. In direct and simple symbols, that independence becomes the metaphor of Harry's killing his own father.

When Harry discovered that his pain about his father's death and his subsequent feelings of inadequacy (he was now fatherless and considered himself less of a person) were really guilt about needing to kill the father that had entered and appropriated his being, he screamed. He screamed: "Dad, *I* killed you because I wanted to kill you. *I* murdered you because I wanted to murder you." And he ended the session with profound sobs of relief.

Harry had made the central philosophic discovery that, in order to be the sanctity that is his center, he must expel all foreign matter. By confusing symbol with reality (the symbol was his father and the reality was his independence) he burdened his life with needless pain and stultifying restrictions. In the philosophic therapy he reached the philosophic foundation of his being and discovered the insight that many wise men have found: He disclosed his consciousness to himself. The calm center, as with a hurricane, exists only after all foreign matter is hurled outside. Harry had discovered the holiness of his center and with that discovery he became a mature adult.

Let us now return to Diana's guilt about her father's death. She must make a parallel discovery. In the simplest language possible, the following points must become clear to her:

1. In objective terms, she is not responsible for her father's death; he is responsible for his daughter's maladjustments. The rightful expectation is that the parent know how to cope with life and produce healthy children.

2. Diana must not ignore or deny her guilt; it is real and important. Negative experiences disclose the truth about humanity — through them persons can be their guilt; move into it; feel and think through it. Diana can do that herself, in part, by deliberately developing fantasies and daydreams about her guilt.

3. By identifying herself with her guilt, Diana moves from guilt as paralysis (neurotic guilt) to guilt as self-disclosure (existential guilt).

4. Her guilt can translate itself into a choice, a decision, a free act, or a deliberate wish. It can be transformed into her decision to fantasy-kill her father, to become an independent freedom, a free inwardness, an ego, and a center. And that decision is one of supreme authenticity. She needs the guilt about her father's death to experience the power of her free-

dom. She herself has freely earned her independence. That is the meaning of her guilt about her father.

The general lessons for you are:

1. You are not responsible for the decisions of others.
2. Guilt is real and important.
3. Be your guilt; identify with it; it will give you strength.
4. Assume fully the responsibility that your guilt suggests. It will make you independent.

But Diana also feels guilty because she is an inadequate mother.

On the basis of the evidence in the letter, Diana *is* inadequate as a mother. She seems to hate her daughter just as much as she obviously hates herself today, hated herself as a child, and perhaps as much as she herself was hated as a child. Her daughter does not exist in her own right as a human being with needs, individuality, and integrity. Diana is not able to see her little girl as an individual any more than her father recognized her right to independence. Why not? Because she does not see herself as an individual. Diana does not think of herself as an inwardness who deserves care, love, and esteem. Apparently, her daughter exists only to satisfy her: "But I am unwilling to give her up now because she is part of me—I am part of her—she is a reminder of my sexuality, my fertility, and selfishly I am unwilling to give that reminder up." Evidently, people are to be used and not to be encountered.

Diana has chosen to deny her daughter, just as she has chosen to deny herself, because in denying her daughter she denies herself as a mother: "I now regret that I did not give her up for adoption."

The facts are clear. Diana has no concept of herself as a subjectivity, an inwardness, a person, or a solid individual. She thinks of herself as a thing; therefore she sees others including her daughter, as objects. Her daughter exists to give her pleasure, just as Diana has existed all these years to give others pleasure. The time has come for her to understand the meaning of *meeting* another consciousness as opposed to *using* that other consciousness; to understand the truth of the principle of love: "As an adult I can choose to meet, confront, witness, understand, and be mirrored by another. I can also choose to love and care for that person." The movement from seeing people as things to that of recognizing them as inward subjectivities is a transformation as dramatic as the evolution from monkey to man.

Here, in the relationship with her daughter, Diana's guilt means far more than proof of the exercise of freedom: She has used her freedom in the most pernicious way of all — to deny herself and another. Being a mother means being Diana — and she has denied being a mother. She has used her freedom to destroy herself! Diana is three things: a woman, a mother, and an ex-child. In denying her own living child she in fact chooses to reject the woman in her; because woman gives birth to child, she chooses to reject the mother in her; and she denies the beauty of being a child — whether that child is herself or her little girl — because she wanted to give up her daughter.

But Diana is *choosing* these denials — they are not automatic. And choosing them is choosing to say *no* to important aspects of life. She is rejecting the principle of life: "My first and last choice is to say *yes* to life." However, if she knows she has the power to say *no*, she knows she also has the power to say *yes*. She must now resolve — and act on the resolve — to ally herself with her womanhood, motherhood, and childhood.

It is, strictly speaking, false to say that Diana is inadequate as a mother, but it is true that she chooses to destroy herself. And that destruction can be the downfall of both Diana and her daughter. Once she perceives her life in this dismal perspective (the destroyer of herself and her daughter) and her previous insights give her the strength and courage to face the bitter truth about herself, she can use the freedom that destroys and change it into a freedom that creates. She must choose herself as a woman-mother-child. She must tell her daughter she loves her and devote her life to making her into a mature and authentic human being.

How does she tell her daughter all these things? By spending time with her, by being rational, tolerant, and affectionate, by being devoted and patient, and by seeing her daughter as an authentic human being. In doing this, she also recreates herself as a mature human being.

Diana's true guilt has been her free denial of the center both in herself and in her daughter. Her task in life now is to reverse that decision and make a total commitment to the authenticity of the center—in herself and in her daughter.

In a sense, Diana's child represents her ultimate challenge. All the guilts of her life are focused on her daughter: On her hinges her adequacy as mother, woman, and even the acceptance of the child she once was. But this focus can also be the source of her answer, which will ascribe ultimate meaning to her life. She will know the meaning of being an important and a needed person.

Generalized, the message to all of us is:

1. Find your true guilt.
2. Devote your life to its correction.

When Diana first became able to express her problem in words, her dilemma was completely intertwined with some of the great problems of human existence. After an existential analysis, she understands that these dilemmas are eternal problems without solutions and that they need not be solved in terms of the problems of everyday existence. This makes it easier for her to deal with her day-to-day problems; she cannot resolve the issue of life and death, but she can choose to say *yes* or *no* to her daughter. The polarities of existence have rendered a choice possible.

Following a class reading and discussion of Diana's letter— anonymous, of course—I received the following communication from a very conservative middle-aged Catholic woman, a member of the class:

Dear Dr. Koestenbaum:

I give you the reverse side of the coin: I have just discovered that my eighteen-year-old daughter has been sleeping with her boyfriend!

Though I have not entertained even the thought of committing suicide (as the father in last Tuesday's letter), I have experienced a feeling that must be closedly related to death. I reached the depths of depression—I wept—and wept—and wept . . . tears of sadness for my daughter's loss of innocence . . . tears of recrimination at what I consider my own failings.

I have been consumed with guilt. I see in phantasm all the little impatiences—the moments of neglect—the times I have been too busy or too tired to listen when she might have needed me. I have failed her.

As a sociology major, I am cognizant of the latest statistics on virginity—almost 80 percent of the sample polled do not consider virginity important. So I am an anachronism. But we have raised our children (my husband and I) in a religion that considers sex a privilege of marriage and holds that premarital sex is sinful. Apparently our daughter is rejecting our values. And of course, she has the right and the free will to make her choice.

When we discussed the situation (she and I) I asked her if she loved her boyfriend or if they had plans to marry. She said he loves her, but she does *not know*—this (of course) made me unhappy for I cannot conceive of sex without love and I see the great proliferation of de-personalized sex in our culture as a threat to the human-ness that places man uniquely above the animal kingdom.

Our daughter now wants to move out—she attended one semester of college and quit. She plans to work (she has a part-time job now and is looking further) and then return to school next fall. She does not wish to get married (I agree with her that she is not mature enough for marriage) but she is so vulnerable and the shyest of all (4) of our children. I gave her *Vitality of Death* to read, the passage about the teenage couple whose sexual attration was overwhelming. She seems to be following one of your alternatives and is seeing her boyfriend infrequently.

This letter is acting as a catharsis—I feel somewhat less anxious simply from having written it. I'm not sure I want you to read it to the class—young people of today are so sophisticated and experienced that I fear their derision. . . .

Very sincerely,
Mrs. Pamela W.

Mrs. W has to confront the dreadful possibility that the value system on which her whole life has been based may be wrong. She comes from an age that may be forever past. That possibility leads to the next insight, that her value system stands or falls by her own affirmation of it. As far as she is concerned, her conservative values are true because *she* says — through her lifestyle — that they are true. They are true exactly as long as she commits her full being to them. That insight is both comforting and frightening; it leads to both peace and vertigo. The metaphysical nature of humankind confirms her freedom — that is supportive. But the metaphysical nature of humankind does not give her any value system whatever, and that fact gives her anxiety.

Mrs. W must learn to lead her own life regardless of her daughter's changes in values. She may have to face the inevitable reality that her daughter will be permanently different from her. That is a consequence of human freedom.

Because of the subjective inwardness of her daughter, which is irreducible, Mrs. W can do little or nothing to change her daughter's lifestyle. Her daughter has the independence of all human beings, and meddling is likely to make everything worse.

Furthermore, Mrs. W must have faith in her daughter and deep respect for the differences between them, according to the principle of individuality. Having faith in her daughter means that she recognizes her daughter's reality. Faith in her daughter is also an expression of love for her. She must think and say, "I am in despair over your way of life. But I fully respect your right to choose for yourself — and I love you for having used that right and chosen freely."

There is, then, something positive Mrs. W can do for her daughter: love her, communicate with her, appreciate her, and share with her — including her own motherly feelings of distress. I have often observed that there is little real intimate and loving (that is, existential and authentic) communication between parents and their children until a crisis arises. Then there is something to communicate about!

Finally, Mrs. W must reaffirm and return to her own religious faith. She must hold on to her own personal integrity. Conservative Catholicism is part of her worldview, and the more intensely she devotes herself to perceiving the world through the eyes of her religion, the more authentic and fulfilled a person she will be.

7

A Program for Self-Development

How can you learn from Diana's insights and apply them to your life? Existential philosophy can help people achieve good mental health when existential insights are quickly translated into therapeutic actions.

By participating in philosophical facilitation you experience a certain amount of growth. You must then capitalize on that growth. You have found a little pearl in your shell which you must now cultivate.

1. You must *understand* what you have achieved. You must conceptualize it, write it down, memorize it, refer to it again and again. You must read about it and write about it. Once conceptualized, the insight has the potential of being permanently rooted in your consciousness. You must be convinced that your participation in this activity has been a genuine act of growth, and that to grow is your true nature. When you grow you will feel healthy and authentic; when you do not grow you may feel depressed and worthless. Always look for growth in every one of your daily activities.

2. You must select an ideal *model*. Your self-concept will guide you through life. If your self-concept is vivid and constant, it will slowly but reliably change you and your world view. You must be intellectually clear about the existential personality theory so that your lifestyle will gradually conform to an authentic human existence. This consideration follows from the principle of responsibility ("I have created and am responsible for the organization of my world; I did not create the raw materials, but I am fully and alone responsible for the social reality that I have constructed around me and the life-

style that I have organized for myself"). You can contribute much to your own happiness by constantly internalizing your ideal self-concept. The child has the parent, hopefully, to serve as model. But we can select our own model and retain its image clearly in the mind.

3. You must *verbalize* your insight. That is accomplished by discussing it. You must make a deliberate effort to seek out friends with whom you can discuss the need for growth and ways of growing. Be aware of the individuals with whom you can discuss your need for growth, and what groups and associations exist in which your growth-need can be discussed. On college and high school campuses, on the job and in the churches, there exist innumerable opportunities for activities in which kindred minds can meet. An individual who seeks authenticity has the responsibility of creating an environment that supports the particular version of his or her quest. It is as easy to modify the environment to suit one's needs and tastes as it is difficult to become authentic unaided, on one's own.

4. You must *experience* your insight. You must not only think and talk, but also experience. You can experience growth in two ways: by *recollection* and by *practice*. To recollect means to experience vicariously past moments of growth: You must list them and feel your way into them so that they appear new and real. Practice means that you must savor each growth experience to make it as large as possible in your experience of your world. A growth experience is like enjoying good food and good wine; you must make yourself fully aware of its flavor, texture, and consistency. Full awareness of each experience of growth will help you to consolidate your gains.

5. You must *integrate* and concretize your growth through habit formation and environmental manipulation. For this, you need a program that will intensify your learning. One way Diana can grow is to lose weight. That can be accomplished successfully only with a complete reorganization of her life: She must learn to enjoy each moment of eating less or of hunger, because these are moments of meaningful growth. She might keep a chart of achievements in weight reduction, small but continuous, and savor repeatedly each one of her suc-

cesses. Furthermore, she must change her environment to remove temptations. She could enroll in a social program of either exercise or weight-watching. She must be conscious at all times of the fact that she is trying to mold her habits and her environment so as to achieve loss of weight. A good model before her eyes will help.

Diana was asked to complete the Insight Application Form. Her answers follow.

INSIGHT APPLICATION FORM

NAME the philosophical insight: The Principle of Growth: *My life is an endless process of growing, emerging and researching out.*

1. *UNDERSTANDING:* Explain the insight in detail: *I have expressed my problems and given them to my teacher. In so doing I have expressed the desire to grow. That desire is part of man's universal nature. Health means continuous growth. To grow means to always move into a real future. I shall choose to always move ahead regardless of difficulties.*

2. *MODEL:* Name a person (living or dead) that you would like to be: *I choose two: Helen of Troy and Helen Keller.*

Now visualize and record how that person exemplifies the philosophic insight: *Helen of Troy reaches out to the world through her beauty. I want to be beautiful like her. I want to have the face that launched a thousand ships. I really believe that if I think I am her I will become more like her. I have always admired Helen Keller. She is strong. She has courage. She never gives up. She conquers all. Imagining I am Helen Keller gives me the strength to do the many difficult things that lie ahead. I enjoy this kind of thinking.*

3. *VERBALIZATIONS:* List opportunities for discussing and sharing the philosophical insight:

(1) *I will make an appointment with Rev. S, and discuss youth groups.*

(2) *I will write a letter to Jane B, who has not heard from me for three years and tell her where I am in life.*

(3) *I will read a child's story about growth to my daughter.*

(4)

4. EXPERIENCES:

A. *RECOLLECTIONS:* List past moments in which the above philosophical insight was experienced:

(1) *I experienced growth when I had my baby.*

(2) *I experienced growth when Mrs. A, my math teacher, told me I was her best student.*

(3) *I experienced growth when I summoned my courage to break up with my boyfriend Tom.*

(4) *I experienced growth when I finally decided to move to a new apartment in a more quiet neighborhood.*

B. *PRACTICE.*

Suggest possible experiences today:

(1) *I will cancel the date for this weekend I made with Bill. I did not want to make that date in the first place.*

(2) *I will today make a much overdue appointment with the dentist.*

(3) *I will start to read today Tillich's* "The Courage to Be."

(4)

5. INTEGRATION: List a program of five steps which will maximize good habits, including a realistic reorganization of your life:

(1) *I will seek psychological counseling. This begins with the search for references.*

(2) *I will find a physician and consult with him about losing weight.*

(3) *I will speak to my teachers about improving my grades and clearing past incomplete courses.*

(4) *I will join a weight-watchers organization. I will first find a list of possible ones in the telephone directory.*

(5) *I will swim three days a week.*

Select an insight that seems real to you. Write it down on the following Insight Application Form. Now develop a program for self-improvement and philosophic growth toward health by filling in the blanks of your form. The task may seem minor and somewhat pedantic; nevertheless, growth occurs in small and manageable stages rather than in grand transformations.

INSIGHT APPLICATION FORM

NAME the philosophical insight:

1. *UNDERSTANDING:* Explain the insight in detail:

2. *MODEL:* Name a person (living or dead) that you would like to be:

Now visualize and record how that person exemplifies the philosophic insight:

3. *VERBALIZATIONS:* List opportunities for discussing and sharing the philosophical insight:

(1)

(2)

(3)

(4)

4. *EXPERIENCES:*

A. *RECOLLECTIONS:* List past moments in which the above philosophical insight was experienced:

(1)

(2)

(3)

(4)

B. *PRACTICE:* Suggest possible experiences today:

(1)

(2)

(3)

(4)

5. *INTEGRATION:* List a program of 5 steps which will maximize good habits, including a realistic reorganization of your life:

   (1)

   (2)

   (3)

   (4)

   (5)

8

The Journal

All of us must learn to like and appreciate ourselves. What practical steps can we take to achieve that? We must develop an answer—a prescription or treatment.

If you are truly interested in a philosophical reconstruction of your life, you will greatly benefit from keeping an intellectual journal or emotional diary. The journal must contain three types of material—all honest. It must include *emotional* (E), *intellectual* or *conceptual* (I), and *fantasy* (F) material.

What, specifically, is journal-writing? It is the ability to *become* the writing. The journal writer must learn to write fast, to *narrow* the space between the fantasy, thought, or feeling and the written word. He or she will soon be able to *think* writing or *write* thinking. Journal-writing is not communication; it is *expression* or *being*. You *are* your writing. In this journal you will work out your destiny. If you are religious, you can view it as a written prayer and you can address it to God, with the understanding that only you and God will know its contents. You may address it to mother or father, or to some other significant person in your life. You may address it to an imaginary or invented person, or to yourself or parts of yourself (such as your rational aspect or your unconscious). The only rule is that it must be both explicit and honest. It must open the floodgates of your inwardness and release its contents for you to see.

You must not throw away the journal, but you need not reread it. Use whatever freedom you have to organize your life in such a way that there will be daily time for your journal. It does not matter that you have extensive entries—what does matter is that you make entries daily. Finally, the journal is not a record of behavior and events but an expression of your emotional and human development. It is *growth* achieved through the written word, and the written word flows like the time that you are (principle C12).

Here is a sample (unedited) from an E-I-F journal shown to me by Bill, one of my students. Bill is nineteen, very bright, rather immature, and a college sophomore. He writes only to be himself honestly, not for effect or communication. In order to facilitate the production of material, I gave him the following assignment: record your (a) fantasies, (b) dreams, (c) ideal self, and (d) real self.

My fantasies are taking over my life. I wonder what it means. Today I plan to record my fantasies and my dreams. I am glad I am writing this journal but must keep it private—at least for a while.

I am going to list my fantasies:

1. I like to think that I am destined to be a profound thinker, a significant contributor to knowledge or art.

2. I wish I had started playing guitar at age 10 instead of age 18. Perhaps I would be a folksinger, a wandering poet, a lonely searching artist.

3. I have often wanted to be a frog-prince capable of any mixture of frogly and human characteristics. I think a human size and intellect would be best with a frog body. As a giant-size frog I would make love to a gypsy princess in *back of* a gondola. It would be beautiful. Wouldn't you like to make love to a giant frog?

4. I sometimes wish that a war would come and I was among the survivors. Then I would work hard to make us all happy in such hard times. Then people would know that I love them. I could prove it to them.

5. To have an independent source of income, an inheritance or something enough to last for the rest of my life. That way I would not have to worry about working. I could travel, write poems, go fishing, paint pictures, make love and fly kites with little kids.

Here are additional and compulsive-like fantasies, desires:

1. I often have urges to caress and kiss perfect strangers, to make love to objects (trees, cars, rocks).

2. I often have urges to break bottles or glasses, to shatter everything into little pieces.

I am now going to record my dreams:

1. I put up a holy brazen plaque to keep out demons, but while I am sleeping the demon comes anyway. I awake and defend myself with my trusty Swiss army pocketknife. I flee to the backyard where there are snakes drowning in mudholes. There are crippled lizards and legless bleeding frogs. Gawking geese guard the only exit to the cobblestone streets of the peaceful town where all are happy. (A cork on the bottle, a mute on the trumpet.).

2. There was a girl who was a cartoon artist. I fell in love with her. Her comic book fantasies swept me away. I had just moved into an old house where a dying Chinaman lived.

The cartoonist girl and I went to the county fair. There was a tough guy there who bumped into me and spilt his coffee. He got mad and asked me (told me) to pay for his coffee. He had been losing his collection of half-dollars through a hole in his pants pocket all day, so when the coffee accident happened he was *really* mad.

This tough guy didn't like the old Chinaman either. He wanted the old man to die and get it over with so he wouldn't have to look at that sick old face anymore.

I moved out of that house where the Chinaman lived and went to look for the cartoonist girl whom I'd lost at the fair.

The following is my Ideal Self:

Tall, slim, healthy, with dark hair. A man who quietly watches his active movements in the world. A man who is aware of the subtle beauty in the hustle-bustle of the everchanging world. A man who can pause to enjoy all the gentle oranges at the corner fruit stand in the sun. A family man with an active career a lovely wife, and three kids. I must never stop growing, never stop learning.

This is my Real Self:

I am skinny, a little too weak. I must move my thoughts outwards more towards others. I find it hard to care for those I do not respect. I only disrespect them because I am repressing a part of myself which is very much like them. I dislike them because I dislike part of myself.

I want to give, but am afraid of being rejected. I don't really see why; in a sense all of us are already rejected. Christ was rejected more than most.

Love is a simple thing. It is only fear that makes it difficult, fear of losing something, fear of losing myself. But those things that I *can* lose are *not* myself.

Anything that is changeable is not really me. I am that power which is able to make change, that power which can lose things (my hair, my job, my reputation, my friends, my personality) and still survive.

I do not know myself very well. I am hidden beneath, behind and amongst a huge mass of "things."

Bill has now become visible: He has expressed — laid out before him — his true nature, for his own self-discovery. He has done it by listing fantasies and dreams and by describing his ideal and his real self.

Let us now return to Diana and follow her program for philosophic reconstruction. By emulating her you can gain pointers on how to use the E-I-F journal for your own personal growth, development, and search for meaning. In addition to wanting self-expression like all of us, she desperately needs to love and be loved. To make that possible, she must use her journal to understand the concept of love and encounter. That can be achieved through the fantasy part of her journal. She can help herself develop this understanding through reading, courses, and through constant writing on the subject. In this way she can even help herself in the absence of another person who loves her.

Love is not just an experience; it is also the understanding of the nature of man and his possibilities. Love is learned conceptually as well as experientially. Again, Diana must use the limited freedom still available to her to give herself an adequate reading list or a sufficient intellectual education on the nature and meaning of love. Because available and relevant books change from time to time and from person to person, it is difficult to give an all-purpose list here. Suggestions that were useful to Diana included Erich Fromm's *The Art of Loving* and Ernesto Cardenal's *To Live Is To Love*.

How can an existential phenomenology help you, as it helped Diana, understand the meaning of love? Here are some suggestions.

To understand the concept of existential encounter and existential love you must understand the difference between, on the one hand, your consciousness, your awareness, your inward and subjective self, your ultimate center, and, on the other hand, your behavior, your personality, your roles, the games you play, and your body. Remember principle A2: "I am a pure consciousness with a psychological personality, a physical body, and many social roles."

You are that subjective consciousness. The religious person discovers that inward consciousness in his or her relation with God. Non-religious persons discover it in searching for the inmost depth of their souls and in the readiness to die and the capacity to give up everything. That is the concept of the first, inner, or transcendental self. We are now ready to define existential love, which is the same as an existential encounter.

An existential encounter is the ability to recognize the consciousness that I am through recognizing the sacred integrity of the consciousness that you are. That relation between two pure consciousnesses I call a transcendental relationship. It can be described as follows, in keeping with the principle of love ("As an adult I can choose to love you and care for you"):

"You are my limit; my land ends where your land begins. Your needs limit my needs. When I recognize in truth and clarity the beautiful and absolute fullness of your existence then I become your limit. I see that your land ends where mine begins and my needs thus limit your needs. You have become a mirror to me and through the purity of that mirror I, for the first time perhaps, discover my own center.

"I can now choose to care for your center; I can choose freely to make a commitment to your center."

Love is thus both a discovery (the mirror) and a decision (the choice of caring). You are now in a position to conceptualize encounter. Let us turn once more to Diana.

Diana has successfully conceptualized the meaning of love as encounter. But she is still alone. Following is an exercise that will help her experience love and assist her in moving out of herself in order to both give and find love. In other words, Diana must *experience* the concept of encounter in order to really understand and then apply it. There are really several exercises that can help her experience the existence of her inward consciousness. First, she must experiment with total *asceticism* (either literally or in fantasy, the latter usually being sufficient) to discover and experience *her own inner self.* Second, she must experiment with total *forgiveness* in order to experience the reality of another pure consciousness. Understanding and being able to imagine a relationship with people on that basic level will give her the idea and the experience of the inner nature of humanity and the real foundation for an authentic encounter relationship.

What is asceticism? It is total denial of the body and the personality. It is the discovery of the silent mind within. Eastern mystics and Western saints have made asceticism a style of life. But for Diana, asceticism was a fantasy exercise only—a guided daydream. Let us follow Diana through her daydream.

Diana first did some exercises for relaxation. I asked her to alternately flex and relax, region by region, all the muscles of her body, beginning with her feet and ending with her facial and head muscles. I suggested to her that she feel warm and glowing all over and then that she feel her heavy weight massively leaning against the surface on which she was resting.

Here is an abbreviated transcription of her *asceticism fantasy.* She spoke every word out loud and made sure that she heard it and that she truly meant what she was saying.

I am hungry. I feel my hunger in my stomach. My stomach hurts; my mouth waters. I want to place a soft candy bar in my mouth and chew it and swallow it.

The hunger is not me. I am not the hunger. The wish to eat is not me; I am not the wish to eat. The hunger is a distant object in the world, like a star in the heavens, like a nest high upon a tree. I am not a hungry self but a self that perceives hunger as some distant thing. The hunger is not me but I can touch the hunger with a long stick.

That pure, empty, silent and observing self is my true inwardness.

I have a bad sore in my mouth. The sore hurts badly; it is getting worse. The sore appears to be closer to my center than my stomach hunger because my mouth is closer to the real "me" than is my stomach. I seem to be centered inside the top of my head, between the eyes. The sore is closer to my center. I am forcing myself not to give a damn about the sore. I don't care if it hurts. I don't care if it gets worse. In fact, I make it hurt by poking it with my finger to practice detachment from it. I don't care if my whole head gets infected, tender, and I die. I really don't care! The sore prevents me from living effectively, but I no longer care about living. I am really able to give up everything! A strange sensation! A freeing experience! A peaceful moment!

The self that gives up life itself and the world with it is my true subjective inwardness, my pure consciousness, my transcendental self.

I want sex. My pelvic region seems to be closer to me than my stomach, since I am sometimes centered in my pelvis. I am sometimes in the eyes and sometimes in the pelvis. Now my center is in the pelvis from which all living movement radiates in waves.

I am now giving up even sex. I am at this moment taking the vow of celibacy. Sex now becomes a distant desire. In fact, desire itself is a thing in the distance; it is no longer me. Desire exists, I perceive it, but is no longer me. I exist at a big distance from even the desires of my pelvis.

That distant self is my true inwardness, my pure consciousness. I've discovered it; I am it; I feel it!

Diana has now made significant progress toward actually experiencing her own true inwardness. It is this part of her that must be recognized by herself and by others as the true Diana.

Her next task is to recognize that pure conscious inwardness in *others*. Then the idea of a transcendental communication or true encounter will finally be accurately understood by her. That is true because encounter is the meeting of two consciousness.

Following is a summary and an edited version of Diana's *forgiveness-fantasy*:

I see a man; I have decided that I want to perceive him not as a body but as another subjective consciousness just like my own. I don't want to see him as a body or as a personality; nor do I wish to see him as being his roles or his physical appearance. I want to see him only as a subjective inwardness. I, therefore, make him ugly in my fantasy. He is ugly everywhere: in the face, the hands, his torso, and his legs. Furthermore, he is dirty, smelly, and generally disgusting. But for all of this I forgive him. I make the religious decision to love him. In forgiving him I perceive the self behind the ugliness and the dirt, and that is his true inward self, precisely like mine. I speak to that self. I say, "Hello, I forgive you and I love you!"

The fantasy gets worse. The man is not only ugly but also evil. His body is evil and so is his behavior and pesonality. He is a mean and vicious criminal. He has done horrible things that deserve only death. In fact, I vomit at the very thought of his evil deeds.

Nevertheless, I shout, "I forgive you!" Behind that atrocious behavior exists the purest self, a center, an inward consciousness cursed with an evil personality. The center is as unaffected by the evil that surrounds it as a rainbow is unaffected by the torrential waterfall over which it hovers. I address myself to that center and say softly this time: "Hello! I forgive you because I love you."

I now experience the true inwardness behind the evil person. That is why I do not believe in the death penalty for even the most heinous criminal. I am able to love the consciousness behind the criminal.

I now perceive a pure ego and through that perception I recognize my own pure ego.

She later recorded both fantasies in her E-I-F journal.

The ascetic forgiving the criminal — that is the model for a transcendental human relationship. Diana has experienced it through fantasy, and her conceptual understanding has thus been increased. She now understands the concept of encounter and the notion of an authentic — transcendental — relationship.

There is an even more profound and accurate way of perceiving the pure ascetic consciousness that is your home: It is the intuition of the silent consciousness, or the consciousness of silence. Silence is not only the absence of noise but also the absence of sights, and above all, the absence of thoughts and ideas. The pure consciousness that you are is total silence and total emptiness. That with which you are in touch when you think of nothing at all is your pure consciousness. That emptiness is accessible to all who are willing to practice meditation. Meditation is most effective when one focuses on nothing at all at moments when it seems least likely or most difficult, such as at times of great excitement or grave pain.

In actual life, Diana had never experienced that kind of a meeting — that is, an encounter of consciousnesses. Her meetings were always bodily. To meet a man meant for Diana to thrust her body on him, or to thrust her role as the "eternal feminine being" on him. Similarly, she expected me to meet her as a body, to perceive her as a body. Her value was her body. To conceive of and experience a transcendental relationship — an existential encounter, a consciousness-to-consciousness meeting — was totally new for her. In short, love was new to her. Love means acceptance and recognition, devotion and care, not performance. Knowledge of the nature of love was one of the most important messages that philosophy could bring to Diana.

Through her obesity, Diana was saying, in effect, "All male-female relationships are physical. I've tried and tried but found no satisfaction. I now make myself unattractive, because the physical encounter is not the real me. But I cannot substitute anything for it, because I do not understand the pure conscious inwardness that I am." In short, Diana needs philosophic education — conceptually and emotionally. She needs to understand and experience her own consciousness and the relationship between consciousness.

You now know the intellectual and emotional meaning of love, or transcendental encounter, and should be able to understand it through experience. Your major task remains: *Express* it now by fully integrating it into your real life.

Diana's next step is to understand how she has failed that model of love in her life. In the past she has not been able to live the idea of a centered self. A centered self is able to love and be loved, and if she has failed in love it is because her center did not exist. Her principal task, therefore, is to build authentic relationships, from her center to that of another. Following are simple and straightforward suggestions for anyone who has difficulty integrating knowledge and understanding with real life.

First, *learn how to build on your already existing strengths.* Do not look for new relationships; rather, strengthen those that are already available. Who are the significant persons in Diana's life? Her daughter, a friend or two, a neighbor, etc. Diana can begin her program for authenticity by loving her daughter and understanding her real needs and by learning in this way to love girlhood and childhood in general.

Meaning and love can be reclaimed most deeply by devotion to a child. This is illustrated in the E-I-F journal of Mary Lou. By rekindling her love for her son, she built on her already existing strengths.

Mary Lou is twenty-three, and has a three-year-old boy, Ian. She is jealous of her husband, who spends much time away from home with his profession as an art teacher.

The following is an excerpt from a letter from Mary Lou:

I wonder most of all about your relationship with your wife. I wonder this because I am a wife whose husband has another love, and you are a husband who has another love. Your love is for philosophy; my husband's love is for art. I feel something like jealousy of you and of my husband because you have found something so important, so all-involving, so much of life. I feel a deep insecurity because I have not found this. I feel a deep fear because I don't believe there is any more for me. I wonder how your wife feels. Perhaps she is not the insecure person that I am, but surely she faces similar problems. What does she do when you are gone nights in a row lecturing, writing, meetings, etc. . .? Does she have something that is just hers, or has she given you all her interest? Has she taken a deep interest in your work, does she like and understand your love of philosophy? I don't really know what I want to know except maybe that there might be people who never find more. For myself, I am not satisfied through my husband's art, and I have not found that something else that's just mine. And I really fear that I won't find it. I am very dissatisfied with myself.

My recommendation to Mary Lou was to seek meaning in her son. She was close to the moment that Tillich called *kairos* (crisis), so that my suggestion properly impressed her as the right solution. She wrote in her journal of her new-found time to be spent with Ian and her renewed devotion for him. The statement and analysis of each one of their new activities together was preceded in her journal by an appropriate photograph. The captions were: "At the Park," "At the Zoo," "Bicycling in the Woods," etc. Her last picture touched me deeply: Mary Lou and Ian waving goodbye to me into the camera.

Mary Lou titles this section of her journal "My Exercise in Living." Her journal is

a free expression of my exercise in living as experienced since the encounter group meeting with Dr. Koestenbaum. At that time I made the decision to live my life by accepting it as the life I have chosen for myself, and also as the best possible life. This has been a very conscious and deliberate decision that has been renewed many times each day. It has not always been a successful decision because I find too little psychical distance between my empirical ego and my consciousness. But the decision is an exercise in living because when it is successful I find great inner peace, and by consciously making the decision to reconstruct my outlook on life each day, in time I hope to be able to make the decision unconsciously, thus having reconstructed my intentionality of consciousness.

Part of the exercise is to relive my childhood through my son, Ian. Together we have learned a great deal in the last several months. It has felt good to be actively involved in play and to return to the joys of childhood. The activity in itself is physically exhausting, but I find myself rejuvenated after our most wild romps. I feel a closeness to him, but also I felt very much in touch with myself.

Riding at Stanford

I woke up saddened on this particular day because my husband had to work, and would not be able to spend the day with Ian and me. I found myself becoming depressed about the lack of time we have together. This is when I made the decision to pack the bike and take a long bike ride with Ian. Besides learning that travel is a symbol for space and time, I have felt the experience of this movement in time. By riding a great distance it is impossible to stay in a depression. It seems that a depression is standing still, is being stagnated, while movement is growth. Although I become very physically tired after riding a great distance, I feel more mentally awake, more rejuvenated, and my physical tiredness feels good. I have known the tiredness and boredom of mental anguish and depression and it feels bad for there is no reason for it. Whenever I feel depression coming on now, I choose to be physically active.

As we rode, I returned to very basic feelings. Ian sang to me, and I felt lucky to have a beautiful child with me. I felt the beauty in the breeze that was cooling me, and in the sounds of the twittering birds. I concentrated on pedaling and on the rhythm of my breathing. I thought of my destination, and the pedaling became easier. Soon it became almost unconscious as if someone else were doing it. This is probably the closest I have come to separating my consciousness and my empirical ego. I felt that I was distant from my body, looking down on myself as if I were not involved in what I was doing.

A later entry reads as follows:

As I watch Ian play on this particular day I find myself feeling a great joy in him. As he climbs the slide he looks to me for approval, and I also feel a great responsibility for him. As I am reconstructing my life I am helping to constitute his, and I now feel that I am doing the best for him I can. I still feel a great inconsistency in dealing with him, but I feel secure even in this inconsistency. It seems that I am learning to accept such inconsistencies as a natural part of life. I understand now what you meant when you said to me that my meaning in life will be found through Ian. While watching him I feel the absolute necessity to respect myself as a person, as a woman, as a wife and as a mother. I feel the need to feel secure in my center. In so finding my center I will be better able to teach Ian this basic love for the humanity of all men, and better able to share love and understanding with Paul, my husband.

And later:

I feel that I have been more understanding of him (my husband, Paul) since my decision to accept my life, for it was also a decision to accept the relationship we have in marriage as meaningful and good. Since the decision to accept, I find that things somehow have changed for the better. I cannot say exactly what that change is except that possibly it is one of viewing the relationship in a completely different light. At any rate, my exercise in living has in no way excluded Paul, even though he has not been with Ian and me on most of our outings. Each time I have gone home with a new "look of love" at the world, at Ian, at Paul, and most of all at myself!

Mary Lou has built on her strengths. Like Diana, she discovered conceptually what an authentic human relationship demands. Then she integrated that knowledge with her life by building on her already-existing strengths: her relationships to her husband and her son. Her success was immediate.

A second suggestion for existential integration is to *learn to identify mature, self-actualizing, and authentic individuals and then relate to them deliberately.* Find out, to the best of your ability, why you may not have been able to do this in the past.

For Diana, previous relationships consisted primarily in using people or in being used. She had two male friends, Jack and Robert. Jack used Diana for sexual purposes only, whereas Robert needed someone for whom he could have contempt and whom he could criticize. Diana willingly lent herself to both of these neurotic purposes. Her real need was for warm and accepting friends, but her reality was cold, cynical, and indifferent. After some philosophic growth, however, she is now alert to her tendency toward inauthentic relationships. She catches herself every time she drifts into a "business" rather than a "personal" relationship.

A third suggestion is to *congregate or live in mature envi-ronments*. Avoid circumstances that are likely to yield inauthentic people, as in a bar, with a neurotic roommate, within a depressing neighborhood or a squelching job. (You can even purchase mature environments—schools and psychotherapy. A therapeutic relationship should be, in many respects, a model human relationship.)

Finally, integration means to be honest in relationships, especially between the sexes. Honesty leads to a relationship of one pure consciousness with another. Honesty can be a device to help two people relate as inward and subjective consciousnesses—in the spirit of true love, care, and mutual understanding, and acceptance rather than merely as two bodies (as in mechanical sex) or two roles (as in a business transaction). In a relationship that demands and tolerates honesty, the basic person is what counts, rather than his superficial accomplishments or visible attributes.

Honest relationships are realistic relationships: No promises are made, even by innuendo, that cannot be kept, and a relationship is maintained only as long as it can be meaningful. In honest relationships an individual is his true self; he plays no games.

Ellen, twenty-eight, an unmarried schoolteacher, is having an affair with a forty-five-year-old man, John, who is married and has three children. John is aggressive, irascible, and a good sexual partner; he drinks excessively, has a very dependent wife and a lifelong history of affairs. Ellen is confused and unhappy because she is totally involved with John: Her life is focused on him, while her future with him is uncertain at best. How would honesty help Ellen?

Honesty points in two directions: you and me. First, Ellen must be honest with herself. She perceives John as filling something like 90 percent of her total life picture, when in reality he can at best occupy only 15 percent of it.

If she is honest, she will admit to herself that John is not available as a future husband, and that he is not accessible even as a good, loyal, and mature friend. He is accessible to Ellen only as a sexual object and a passing companion. If she sees him as 90 percent of her world, she is dishonest with her-self; if she sees him as 15 percent of her total world, she is hon-est. (It would also be dishonest to see him as 0 percent of her world, for she cannot give him up.) So much for honesty with herself.

Honesty with John is another matter. She thought it her duty to be 100 percent honest with John, but total honesty with him is in this case impossible. Partial honesty may be indicated but is not essential. Because John is 15 percent of her world, she owes him exactly this percentage of sharing. In other words, by being fully honest with John she was really being dishonest with herself, pretending he was something he was not. What Ellen does need desperately, however, is to establish an honest relationship with a man who can and will recipro-cate. She needs a 100 percent relationship.

In simple English, Ellen needs a friend first and a sexual partner second. She has a history of meeting men superficially and sexually. Her first value is sexual. Later, after sex, she tries openness—which then fails. I suggested to her she do the reverse, telling her that she has not yet met the man she wants to marry because she has had no experience or practice in meeting men on an honest, open, and mature person-to-person, rather than body-to-body, level. She must start rela-tionships with honest confrontation and open meeting. Once a transcendental connection has been established, she can take the sexual initiative herself if necessary. An authentic woman attracts the man she wants through her authenticity, not through her body and her sexual competence.

Honesty cannot be achieved with the immature, because a person must first be honest with himself before honesty with a lover makes any sense. The corollary of this insight is that love is not for children but for adults—and adulthood is more like-ly to begin in the middle thirties than in the teens!

The following activities will help you gain further benefits from this chapter:

1. Select the three themes from the Master Table that are the most relevant to your life.

2. Develop an Insight Application Form for each of these themes.

3. Start an E-I-F journal.

4. After you have made some progress with these exercises, begin formulating in your journal a program for the *integration* of your insights, as was done by Mary Lou.

Remember that your self-disclosure is of two kinds: individual and philosophical (theme B of the Master Table). Therefore, your integration must not be limited to the psychological insights you may have about your personality structure, but must extend to the philosophic insights that apply to all human beings. Remember also that many of your problems are due to the fact that you are a human being and not due to an illness that afflicts only selected persons.

5. As a corollary to No. 4 above, answer specifically these questions, by discussing them in your E-I-F journal:

a. How can I build on my strengths?

b. Whom do I know who is authentic? How can I relate to him (her, them)?

c. Is my environment mature? If not, how can I change it?

d. Am I honest with myself? With others? How can I improve in being honest?

PART 2

Pain

In Part One we discussed the general outlines of an existential personality theory as it follows from a development of the concept of consciousness. Several applications were suggested primarily to show the usefulness of the theory for personal development, but also to illustrate the proper nature of that theory of consciousness.

In Part Two we undertake an extensive application of that theory for the understanding and management of pain in many of its forms.

9

The Pain Test

Pain does not mean physical suffering alone. I use the word "pain" to stand for the generalized experience of negation or negativity in life—from anxiety to guilt and from depression to bodily pain. The Pain Test will provide a measure of how much negation you experience in your life as compared to negation that others experience. In addition, the test discriminates among eight different types of pain. By taking the test you can develop a kind of personal "pain profile" or "negation profile" that you will find very useful.

What is your "pain mass" and your "pain profile"? This test, like all the others in this book, is not a psychological instrument, strictly speaking. It is simply an exercise to aid your self-understanding and philosophical discussion.

Here is a list of 285 adjectives. If you do not know the meaning of a word, look it up in the dictionary. Work fast. Decide for each adjective whether it *describes you* at this moment (T or +), or whether it *does not describe you* at this moment (F or 0). Then use the sheets following to get your totals.

1. accepted____	12. alienated____	23. asinine____
2. accomplished____	13. alive____	24. atrophied____
3. achieving____	14. alone____	25. attractive____
4. aching____	15. ambiguous____	26. authentic____
5. adult____	16. ambivalent____	27. awed____
6. affectionate____	17. angry____	28. awful____
7. afraid____	18. annoyed____	29. bad____
8. aggravated____	19. anxious____	30. bitter____
9. aggressive____	20. appreciated____	31. blue____
10. agitated____	21. arthritic____	32. bored____
11. aimless____	22. ashamed____	33. bouncy____

34. breathless____
35. bright____
36. broken____
37. burning____
38. callous____
39. capable____
40. choking____
41. comfortable____
42. confident____
43. conflicting____
44. confused____
45. contemptible____
46. contradictory____
47. cramped____
48. creative____
49. crippled____
50. crucified____
51. cruel____
52. crying____
53. dead____
54. defeated____
55. defective____
56. deficient____
57. depressed____
58. desirable____
59. desperate____
60. destroyed____
61. destructive____
62. different____
63. difficult____
64. diffident____
65. dignified____
66. disappointed____
67. discouraged____
68. disgusted____
69. disinterested____
70. distant____
71. dizzy____
72. dreadful____
73. dry____
74. dull____
75. dying____
76. ecstatic____
77. embarrassed____
78. embittered____
79. emphatic____
80. empty____

81. esteemed____
82. evil____
83. exhausted____
84. exuberant____
85. fabulous____
86. failing____
87. fantastic____
88. feeble____
89. fenced in____
90. feverish____
91. foolish____
92. foreign____
93. fragmented____
94. free____
95. frenzied____
96. friendly____
97. frustrated____
98. furious____
99. gleeful____
100. good____
101. grounded____
102. growing____
103. grown up____
104. guilty____
105. handcuffed____
106. handsome____
107. happy____
108. hard____
109. hateful____
110. hating____
111. healthy____
112. helpless____
113. hemmed in____
114. hindered____
115. hollow____
116. homeless____
117. hostile____
118. humorless____
119. hungry____
120. idiotic____
121. ill____
122. imbecilic____
123. immature____
124. impassive____
125. impeded____
126. imprisoned____
127. inadequate____

128. inappropriate____
129. inauthentic____
130. inconsequential____
131. incredible____
132. independent____
133. indifferent____
134. individual____
135. ineffective____
136. ineffectual____
137. inexperienced____
138. insane____
139. inspired____
140. insubstantial____
141. intelligent____
142. irreplaceable____
143. isolated____
144. itchy____
145. jailed____
146. joyful____
147. judged____
148. jumpy____
149. kind____
150. liked____
151. limited____
152. lonely____
153. lost____
154. loved____
155. loving____
156. low____
157. mad____
158. mature____
159. mean____
160. meaningless____
161. mistaken____
162. murderous____
163. nauseous____
164. negative____
165. nervous____
166. non-existent____
167. nonsensical____
168. odd____
169. out-of-place____
170. pained____
171. painful____
172. panicked____
173. paradoxical____
174. paralyzed____

175. passionate____
176. pathetic____
177. peaceful____
178. petrified____
179. philosophical____
180. pleasant____
181. pleased____
182. pointless____
183. positive____
184. punished____
185. purposeful____
186. purposeless____
187. rebellious____
188. recognized____
189. rejected____
190. relaxed____
191. removed____
192. respected____
193. restricted____
194. rewarded____
195. rheumatoid____
196. ridiculous____
197. rooted____
198. rude____
199. sad____
200. sadistic____
201. safe____
202. sane____
203. screaming____
204. self-actualizing____
205. self-conscious____
206. self-pitying____
207. self-reliant____
208. separated____
209. sexless____
210. sexy____
211. shaken____

212. shameful____
213. shy____
214. sick____
215. sinful____
216. sleepy____
217. slowed down____
218. smart____
219. smiling____
220. sore____
221. sorrowful____
222. spent____
223. split____
224. stagnant____
225. stoical____
226. stopped____
227. strong____
228. stupid____
229. successful____
230. suffocating____
231. suicidal____
232. supported____
233. taut____
234. tender____
235. tense____
236. terrified____
237. thirsty____
238. tight____
239. tired____
240. tolerant____
241. torn____
242. tragic____
243. twisted____
244. ugly____
245. ulcerated____
246. unappreciated____
247. unattached____
248. unattractive____

249. unbelievable____
250. unclear____
251. unconcerned____
252. uncreative____
253. undecided____
254. undeserving____
255. undesirable____
256. unfair____
257. unfeeling____
258. unfree____
259. unimaginative____
260. unique____
261. unjust____
262. unkind____
263. unloved____
264. unreal____
265. unresolved____
266. unspirited____
267. unworthy____
268. uprooted____
269. vacuous____
270. valueless____
271. vanished____
272. vibrant____
273. vicious____
274. vigorous____
275. vile____
276. violent____
277. warm____
278. weak____
279. weakened____
280. weeping____
281. whole____
282. worthless____
283. wrenched____
284. wrong____
285. youthful____

Pain Test Score Sheet (Total Score)
The "correct" answers for all items of the Pain Test follow.
Place a check (✔) after each correct answer.

1 F 0 _____	41 F 0 _____	81 F 0 _____	121 T + _____
2 F 0 _____	42 F 0 _____	82 T + _____	122 T + _____
3 F 0 _____	43 T + _____	83 T + _____	123 T + _____
4 T + _____	44 T + _____	84 F 0 _____	124 T + _____
5 F 0 _____	45 T + _____	85 F 0 _____	125 T + _____
6 F 0 _____	46 T + _____	86 T + _____	126 T + _____
8 T + _____	47 T + _____	87 F 0 _____	127 T + _____
9 T + _____	48 F 0 _____	88 T + _____	128 T + _____
10 T + _____	49 T + _____	89 T + _____	129 T + _____
11 T + _____	50 T + _____	90 T + _____	130 T + _____
12 T + _____	52 T + _____	91 T + _____	131 F 0 _____
13 F 0 _____	53 T + _____	92 T + _____	132 F 0 _____
14 T + _____	54 T + _____	93 T + _____	133 T + _____
15 T + _____	55 T + _____	94 F 0 _____	134 F 0 _____
16 T + _____	56 T + _____	96 F 0 _____	135 T + _____
17 T + _____	57 T + _____	97 T + _____	136 T + _____
18 T + _____	58 F 0 _____	98 T + _____	137 T + _____
19 T + _____	59 T + _____	99 F 0 _____	138 T + _____
20 F 0 _____	60 T + _____	100 F 0 _____	140 T + _____
21 T + _____	61 T + _____	101 F 0 _____	141 F 0 _____
22 T + _____	62 T + _____	102 F 0 _____	142 F 0 _____
23 T + _____	63 T + _____	103 F 0 _____	143 T + _____
24 T + _____	64 T + _____	104 T + _____	144 T + _____
25 F 0 _____	65 F 0 _____	105 T + _____	145 T + _____
26 F 0 _____	66 T + _____	106 F 0 _____	146 F 0 _____
27 T + _____	67 T + _____	107 F 0 _____	147 T + _____
28 T + _____	68 T + _____	108 F 0 _____	148 T + _____
29 T + _____	69 T + _____	109 T + _____	149 F 0 _____
30 T + _____	70 T + _____	110 T + _____	150 F 0 _____
31 T + _____	71 T + _____	111 F 0 _____	151 T + _____
32 T + _____	72 T + _____	112 T + _____	152 T + _____
33 F 0 _____	73 T + _____	113 T + _____	153 T + _____
34 T + _____	74 T + _____	114 T + _____	154 F 0 _____
35 F 0 _____	75 T + _____	115 T + _____	155 F 0 _____
36 T + _____	76 F 0 _____	116 T + _____	156 T + _____
37 T + _____	77 T + _____	117 T + _____	157 T + _____
38 T + _____	78 T + _____	118 T + _____	158 F 0 _____
39 F 0 _____	79 F 0 _____	119 T + _____	159 T + _____
40 T + _____	80 T + _____	120 T + _____	160 T + _____

161 T + __	201 F 0 _____	241 T + _____	281 F 0 _____
162 T + __	202 F 0 _____	242 T + _____	282 T + _____
163 T + __	203 T + _____	243 T + _____	283 T + _____
164 T + __	204 F 0 _____	244 T + _____	284 T + _____
165 T + _____	205 T + _____	245 T + _____	285 F 0 _____
166 T + _____	206 T + _____	246 T + _____	
167 T + _____	207 F 0 _____	247 T + _____	
168 T + _____	208 T + _____	248 T + _____	
169 T + _____	209 T + _____	249 F 0 _____	
170 T + _____	210 F 0 _____	250 T + _____	
171 T + _____	211 T + _____	251 T + _____	
172 T + _____	212 T + _____	252 T + _____	
173 T + _____	213 T + _____	253 T + _____	
174 T + _____	214 T + _____	254 T + _____	
175 F 0 _____	215 T + _____	255 T + _____	
176 T + _____	216 T + _____	256 T + _____	
177 F 0 _____	217 T + _____	257 T + _____	
178 T + _____	218 F 0 _____	258 T + _____	
179 T + _____	219 F 0 _____	259 T + _____	
180 F 0 _____	220 T + _____	260 F 0 _____	
181 F 0 _____	221 T + _____	261 T + _____	
182 T + _____	222 T + _____	262 T + _____	
183 F 0 _____	223 T + _____	263 T + _____	
184 T + _____	224 T + _____	264 T + _____	
185 F 0 _____	225 T + _____	265 T + _____	
186 T + _____	226 T + _____	266 T + _____	
187 T + _____	227 F 0 _____	267 T + _____	
188 F 0 _____	228 T + _____	268 T + _____	
189 T + _____	229 F 0 _____	269 T + _____	
190 F 0 _____	230 T + _____	270 T + _____	
191 T + _____	231 T + _____	271 T + _____	
192 F 0 _____	232 F 0 _____	272 F 0 _____	
193 T + _____	233 T + _____	273 T + _____	
194 F 0 _____	234 F 0 _____	274 F 0 _____	
195 T + _____	235 T + _____	275 T + _____	
196 T + _____	236 T + _____	276 T + _____	
197 F 0 _____	237 T + _____	277 F 0 _____	
198 T + _____	238 T + _____	278 T + _____	
199 T + _____	239 T + _____	279 T + _____	
200 T + _____	240 F 0 _____	280 T + _____	

Number of "correct" answers
This is your total score.

Pain Test Score Sheet (Partial Score)
The *"correct" answer in* all items *of the CW (contrasting*
words) scale is F or 0.

Item Number	Your Answer Was	Check (✔) If Correct
1	_____	_____
2	_____	_____
3	_____	_____
5	_____	_____
6	_____	_____
13	_____	_____
20	_____	_____
25	_____	_____
26	_____	_____
33	_____	_____
35	_____	_____
39	_____	_____
41	_____	_____
42	_____	_____
48	_____	_____
58	_____	_____
65	_____	_____
76	_____	_____
79	_____	_____
81	_____	_____
84	_____	_____
85	_____	_____
87	_____	_____
94	_____	_____
96	_____	_____
99	_____	_____
100	_____	_____
101	_____	_____
102	_____	_____
103	_____	_____
106	_____	_____
107	_____	_____
111	_____	_____
131	_____	_____
132	_____	_____
134	_____	_____
139	_____	_____
141	_____	_____
142	_____	_____
146	_____	_____
149	_____	_____

Pain Test Score Sheet (cont.)

150	____	____
154	____	____
155	____	____
158	____	____
175	____	____
177	____	____
180	____	____
181	____	____
183	____	____
185	____	____
188	____	____
190	____	____
192	____	____
194	____	____
197	____	____
201	____	____
202	____	____
204	____	____
207	____	____
210	____	____
218	____	____
219	____	____
227	____	____
229	____	____
232	____	____
234	____	____
240	____	____
249	____	____
260	____	____
272	____	____
274	____	____
277	____	____
281	____	____
285	____	____

Number of "correct" answers.
This is your score on the CW scale.
Now plot it on your Pain Profile.

Mark your totals on the following two scales in order to interpret your general pain score. We should assume that the more intense your perceived pain, the more useful the discussion on pain will be for you. Pain can be an asset to fulfillment in life.

Total Score

    You perceive yourself as:

      A very unhappy negative person. 157

                                        135

      An unhappy person 113

                                        92

      An average person. 70

                                        48

      A happy person. 26

                                        5

      A very happy positive person . . . .

CW (contrasting words, or pleasure) Score

    How intense is your experience of joy?

      Far below average 46

                                        40

      Below average. 34

                                        28

      Average 22

                                        15

      Above average 9

                                        3

      Far above average . . . .

Now proceed to develop your Pain Profile. Use the following worksheets to ascertain your partial scores. You will receive a score for each of eight types of pain or negative experiences — from frustration (F-scale) to meaninglessness (M-scale). Then plot your profile in the Pain Profile blank provided.

Pain Test Score Sheet (Partial Score)
The "correct" answer in all *items of the F (frustration) scale is*
T or +.

Item Number	Your Answer Was	Check (✔) If Correct
8	_____	_____
9	_____	_____
17	_____	_____
18	_____	_____
29	_____	_____
30	_____	_____
36	_____	_____
50	_____	_____
51	_____	_____
54	_____	_____
61	_____	_____
63	_____	_____
68	_____	_____
78	_____	_____
82	_____	_____
89	_____	_____
97	_____	_____
98	_____	_____
105	_____	_____
110	_____	_____
112	_____	_____
113	_____	_____
114	_____	_____
117	_____	_____
125	_____	_____
126	_____	_____
145	_____	_____
151	_____	_____
157	_____	_____
159	_____	_____
162	_____	_____
187	_____	_____
193	_____	_____
198	_____	_____
200	_____	_____
203	_____	_____
217	_____	_____
226	_____	_____
258	_____	_____
262	_____	_____
273	_____	_____

Pain Test Score Sheet (cont.)

275   _____   _____
276   _____   _____

Total number of "correct" answers.
This is your score on the F scale.   →
Now plot it on your Pain Profile.

Pain Test Score Sheet (Partial Score)
The "correct" answer in all *items of the* **P** *(physical pain) scale*
is T or +.

Item Number	*Your Answer Was*	*Check (✔) If Correct*
4	_____	_____
21	_____	_____
24	_____	_____
34	_____	_____
37	_____	_____
40	_____	_____
47	_____	_____
49	_____	_____
71	_____	_____
90	_____	_____
119	_____	_____
121	_____	_____
144	_____	_____
163	_____	_____
170	_____	_____
171	_____	_____
174	_____	_____
195	_____	_____
214	_____	_____
220	_____	_____
230	_____	_____
237	_____	_____
245	_____	_____
279	_____	_____

Total number of "correct" answers
This is your score on the P scale.   →
Now plot it on your Pain Profile.

Pain Test Score Sheet (Partial Score)
The "correct" answer in all *items of the A (anxiety and dread)*
scale is T or +.

Item Number	Your Answer Was	Check (✔) If Correct
7	_____	_____
10	_____	_____
19	_____	_____
27	_____	_____
28	_____	_____
59	_____	_____
60	_____	_____
72	_____	_____
95	_____	_____
116	_____	_____
148	_____	_____
153	_____	_____
165	_____	_____
172	_____	_____
178	_____	_____
189	_____	_____
208	_____	_____
211	_____	_____
233	_____	_____
235	_____	_____
236	_____	_____
238	_____	_____
263	_____	_____
268	_____	_____

Total number of "correct" answers
This is your score on the A scale.
Now plot it on your Pain Profile.

Pain Test Score Sheet (Partial Score)
The "correct" answer in all *items of the L (loneliness) scale is T*
or +.

Item Number	Your Answer Was	Check (✔) If Correct
12	_____	_____
14	_____	_____

Pain Test Score Sheet (cont.)

62	_____	_____
70	_____	_____
77	_____	_____
80	_____	_____
91	_____	_____
92	_____	_____
115	_____	_____
116	_____	_____
128	_____	_____
137	_____	_____
143	_____	_____
147	_____	_____
152	_____	_____
153	_____	_____
168	_____	_____
169	_____	_____
189	_____	_____
191	_____	_____
196	_____	_____
205	_____	_____
206	_____	_____
208	_____	_____
247	_____	_____
268	_____	_____
269	_____	_____

Total number of "correct" answers
This is your score on the L scale.
Now plot it on your Pain Profile.

Pain Test Score Sheet (Partial Score)
The "correct" answer in all items of the T (tragedy and conflict) scale is T or + .

Item Number	Your Answer Was	Check (✔) If Correct
15	_____	_____
16	_____	_____
43	_____	_____
44	_____	_____
46	_____	_____
52	_____	_____

Pain Test Score Sheet (cont.)

93	_____	_____
173	_____	_____
199	_____	_____
221	_____	_____
223	_____	_____
233	_____	_____
235	_____	_____
238	_____	_____
241	_____	_____
242	_____	_____
243	_____	_____
250	_____	_____
253	_____	_____
265	_____	_____
280	_____	_____
283	_____	_____

Total number of "correct" answers
This is your score on the T scale.
Now plot it on your Pain Profile.

Pain Test Score Sheet (Partial Score)
The "correct" answer in all *items of the G (guilt) scale is T or +.*

Item Number	Your Answer Was	Check (✔) If Correct
22	_____	_____
23	_____	_____
24	_____	_____
55	_____	_____
56	_____	_____
60	_____	_____
66	_____	_____
82	_____	_____
91	_____	_____
104	_____	_____
120	_____	_____
122	_____	_____
129	_____	_____

Pain Test Score Sheet (cont.)

147	————	————
161	————	————
176	————	————
184	————	————
196	————	————
212	————	————
215	————	————
228	————	————
254	————	————
256	————	————
261	————	————
267	————	————
282	————	————
284	————	————

Total number of "correct" answers
This is your score on the G scale.
Now plot it on your Pain Profile.

Pain Test Score Sheet (Partial Score)
The "correct" answer in all *items of the D (depression) scale is*
T or +.

Item Number	Your Answer Was	Check (✔) If Correct
11	————	————
31	————	————
45	————	————
49	————	————
53	————	————
57	————	————
64	————	————
67	————	————
69	————	————
75	————	————
77	————	————
83	————	————

Pain Test Score Sheet (cont.)

86	_____	_____
88	_____	_____
109	_____	_____
118	_____	_____
123	_____	_____
127	_____	_____
129	_____	_____
130	_____	_____
135	_____	_____
136	_____	_____
138	_____	_____
156	_____	_____
164	_____	_____
166	_____	_____
176	_____	_____
182	_____	_____
186	_____	_____
199	_____	_____
205	_____	_____
209	_____	_____
213	_____	_____
216	_____	_____
231	_____	_____
239	_____	_____
242	_____	_____
244	_____	_____
246	_____	_____
248	_____	_____
251	_____	_____
252	_____	_____
255	_____	_____
266	_____	_____
267	_____	_____
271	_____	_____
278	_____	_____
282	_____	_____

Total number of "correct" answers
This is your score on the D scale.
Now plot it on your Pain Profile.

Pain Test Score Sheet (Partial Score)
The "correct" answer in all *items of the M (meaninglessness)*
scale is T or +.

Item *Number*	*Your* *Answer Was*	*Check (✔)* *If Correct*
11	——	——
32	——	——
38	——	——
53	——	——
67	——	——
69	——	——
73	——	——
74	——	——
80	——	——
108	——	——
115	——	——
116	——	——
124	——	——
130	——	——
133	——	——
135	——	——
136	——	——
138	——	——
140	——	——
160	——	——
166	——	——
167	——	——
174	——	——
179	——	——
182	——	——
222	——	——
224	——	——
225	——	——
257	——	——
259	——	——
264	——	——
268	——	——
269	——	——
270	——	——
271	——	——

Total number of "correct" answers
This is your score on the M scale.
Now plot it on your Pain profile.

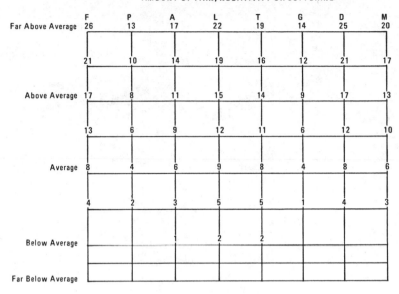

PAIN PROFILE
AMOUNT OF PAIN, NEGATIVITY OR SUFFERING

	F	P	A	L	T	G	D	M
Far Above Average	26	13	17	22	19	14	25	20
	21	10	14	19	16	12	21	17
Above Average	17	8	11	15	14	9	17	13
	13	6	9	12	11	6	12	10
Average	8	4	6	9	8	4	8	6
	4	2	3	5	5	1	4	3
Below Average			1	2	2			
Far Below Average								

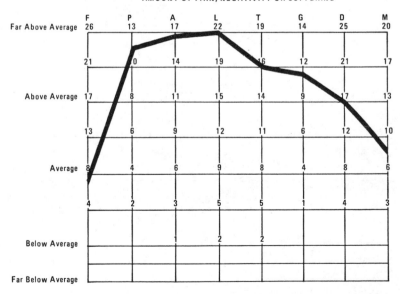

PAIN PROFILE
AMOUNT OF PAIN, NEGATIVITY OR SUFFERING

	F	P	A	L	T	G	D	M
Far Above Average	26	13	17	22	19	14	25	20
	21	10	14	19	16	12	21	17
Above Average	17	8	11	15	14	9	17	13
	13	6	9	12	11	6	12	10
Average	8	4	6	9	8	4	8	6
	4	2	3	5	5	1	4	3
Below Average			1	2	2			
Far Below Average								

129

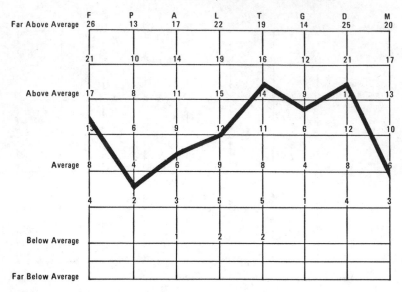

PAIN PROFILE
AMOUNT OF PAIN, NEGATIVITY OR SUFFERING

PAIN PROFILE
AMOUNT OF PAIN, NEGATIVITY OR SUFFERING

130

Your profile will suggest to you which areas of pain or negation are most intense in your life. Those sections dealing with
your higher-intensity negative experiences or pains may then
be the most useful ones for you. For example, Figure 1 represents an individual with somewhat high manifest pain in life.
In fact, his total score is 107, which defines him as an unhappy
person. His CW score is 15, which makes him a person of
slightly above average manifest joy. The therapeutic strategy
suggested by his profile is to focus on at least the exploration of
anxiety and loneliness as the source of his meaning in life. The
unique cognitive character of these two emotions is likely to be
his most effective entry into philosophical depth and emotional authenticity. This person is not frustrated and seems to
find his life quite meaningful. He does have a syndrome of
physical pain, anxiety, loneliness (above all), conflict (T),
guilt, and some depression. That sequence does in fact describe that person's being-in-the-world quite accurately.

Now look at Figure 2. Here we find less pain. Nevertheless,
the cluster of manifest negation in this person's life is found in
the areas of tragedy, guilt, and depression. These are the pains
that are to be discussed and examined first. It is in these pains
that the individual will be most helped by and responsive to
philosophical insights about the meaning of his life. This person has practically no physical pain; his life seems quite meaningful to him. He has a low level of anxiety, but there is a little
loneliness and some frustration in his life.

Finally, in Figure 3 we find a very happy person. Nevertheless, if we want to discuss his life philosophically, we are urged
by his responses to focus on his experience of anxiety. This person has no physical pain, is not in the least depressed or frustrated. He is slightly lonely and has some conflict but no guilt,
just some anxiety. That describes the meaning of negation in
his life.

10

What Is Pain?

Ted is an unmarried thirty-one-year-old high-school history teacher. He has a splendid grasp of the existential process which finds in the depths of despair the answer to life's psychological problems. He shows us the truth of the first great existential insight about pain: That it discloses to us regions deeply buried, to which we have scant access without this maturing catharsis. Here is an eloquent record, taken from his journal, of the catharsis of Ted's feelings. He allows us to witness the transformation from depression to joy, from anxiety to peace, and from despair to hope. The statement is worth reading in its entirety. It will put us in touch with the experience of pain.

The ideas expressed in this journal resulted from situations in which I was deeply involved in life. These experiences were filled with intense emotions of depair and joy as I climbed out of a darkened pit in which I felt helplessly lost and void of meaning to a point where I seemed to be one with God.

These personal encounters deal with problems that are of concern to existentialism, the meaninglessness of existence, the purposelessness of man's life, man's struggle to find meaning while being caught up in nothingness, the threat of non-being, and finally, the discovery of man's ultimate freedom to confer value on his life. I have come to grips with these problems through intense encounters with life.

January 19

I am alone, desperately, painfully alone. Is there any purpose or meaning to my life? Is there an ultimate direction for me to discover? Why am I dissatisfied with my present existence? Is there no way to

132

still this passionate urge to be something more than what I am? My mind is disjointed, disorganized; I am losing contact with myself.

Nothing seems to hold meaning for me anymore, at least not the kind of meaning that satisfies me. I realize that as a teacher I'm expendable, the school system can function without me, my students will miss me for a while, but I doubt that any child's life has been profoundly affected by my teaching or by my personality. My friends and loved ones can live without me. I want to have meaning for others, and it is only a supreme position of importance with which I will be satisfied and right now I am without importance.

At times I have perceived my seemingly infinite potential. I have caught glimpses of what it is to be God. It is this identification with God that I seek, this ultimate unity rests dormant within my soul and I feel compelled to give it life for it is the source of my meaning. Will I ever find this meaning which I so desperately seek? Oh, God, the futility of my search, the impotency of my mortal mind, how can I find you, how can I be united with the infinite Thou?

The thought of my separateness, my absolute distinction eats away at me. I begin to feel threatened for I have always had faith in the existence of ultimate meaning and purpose. It has always seemed to me that my loneliness could be overcome, but I have never found the way. Now, more so than ever before, I realize that I stand alone on this planet. God seems far off, even nonexistent.

I feel that I am forced into this position of loneliness and I rebel against having no choice in the matter. Yes, it's my freedom, my absolute independence that frightens me. I was placed here without having any say, and I was put here alone, and for what reason, what purpose do I have? I desperately want my meaning and purpose to be made clear to me. I want to understand—what is the niche I am destined to fill? Life would be so much easier if it were programmed, if meaning and purpose were built into me. Why can't I understand? Why did God leave it up to me to discover what I am? My freedom, my absolute independence terrifies me. I want to escape from my predicament but I can't, I'm trapped!

I have no meaning, God has left me alone, I am deathly afraid that without meaning I will be nothing. Tears of desperation flow down my cheeks. Violently I sob, meaning and purpose have been drained from me, I sink into total despair and absolute isolation, I am nothing! I realize finally and absolutely that no outside relationship can change the fact that I can only be alone, distinct and separate. No matter how I try to overcome my isolation, whether through means of loving God, man, woman or other, I am still alone. I must realize and accept this fact of my existence.

I now feel completely drained of emotion. The tears cease, I lie still as a wonderful calm sweeps over me. My thoughts have ceased for I am void of meaning and purpose, thought has no function, I have no function, no purpose, I am empty, I am nothing.

I feel relieved and somehow satisfied. A flash of insight illuminates my world. I begin to feel self-confident, a new vitality wells up in my being. I realize that my mistake has been to seek meaning outside of my life. How has this obvious truth eluded me for so long! It's been right before my eyes. No, that is the very reason that the truth, my truth, has eluded me. I relied on the information which my senses have brought to me; I've based my knowledge of reality only on what I could see, hear, taste and smell. Because I've neglected the *subject* of my experience, I've gone outside the source from which my perceptions emanate. Of course I'm empty of meaning, if I had meaning built into my life then I wouldn't be able to direct my own life, I would be determined by forces which I couldn't control, I would have no free choice. It is the very fact of my absolute aloneness that gives me the ultimate power and freedom that I seek. In my uniqueness and individuality rests the true value and meaning of myself, in this separateness I find my freedom.

I now begin to understand, to really understand, the true meaning of myself. I understand that my absolute separateness is the reason for my freedom. I understand that outside approval and acceptance is not necessary for my survival.

Absurd visions begin to play in my mind, visions of a fool attempting to find his place in life by seeking the acceptance of others who have no idea where they are in life. I see a world of fools leading each other around in a blind attempt to hide from their true nature. I see fools pursuing meaningless goals which they believe will help them overcome the separateness they fear but the separateness and emptiness which in actuality is the very source of their freedom.

I laugh uproariously at the irony of the panorama that unfolds before me. The tears stream down my face; never before have I laughed so hard. What a tremendous feeling, what a tremendous relief. I feel purged and gloriously free. I think not of my separateness, but of my freedom. This realization of the real meaning of my isolation has freed me of the categories in which others have placed me, and in which I have placed myself. I am freed of the bonds of status and prestige. I am no longer threatened, for what I was threatened by before doesn't exist. I realize now that I am the source of my own value; I cannot gain value and direction from factors outside myself in the way I once perceived.

My true self is coming to fruition. I am discovering myself by realizing what I am not. I am not a teacher, a son, a lover, a philosopher, not even a man. In a way I am all these people, but I am also much more, infinitely more, and I must not limit my essence to the idea of these illusions. I can lose my job, my house, my lover, and I will still be here.

I laugh at myself for what I have often thought of my self as being. I laugh at the absurdity of seeking identity through the possession of status and material possessions. The freedom that I have always sought is right here! What a wonderful thought, I seek myself and here I am.

I must not hold on so tightly to the things I once thought were responsible for giving meaning and value to my life. My job, possessions, friends, lovers and even my ideas have been grasped so tightly that my life has been strangled. Relaxation is so important! By releasing my grip on life I allow true experience to filter through.

I feel close to God. The loneliness I felt before was caused by the fact that I was seeking identity and security by trying to possess things and ideas which I believed were essential aspects of my self but in reality were far removed from the consciousness which I realized myself to be. My loneliness was an extreme reaction against trying to unite with things foreign to my nature.

Again I am filled with emotion, only these tears that burst forth are tears of joy. I fall on my knees, throw up my arms to heaven and cry out my thanks to God for my freedom. I delight in the pure joy of mere being. At last I am at peace with myself and with the idea that God is the supreme conscious awareness that I am.

January 20

What an exhilarating experience to be totally involved in life. Whenever I encounter the basic problems of life head-on, regardless of the emotions I feel at the time, I always come out of the experience feeling charged with energy, self-confident and with a positive attitude toward life.

My involvement with the eternal present has enabled me to contact the real meaning of my existence. I realize the importance of concentrating on the present moment. A diffused mind that is filled with value judgments and presuppositions wanders to and fro from past to future missing reality completely.

Ted, with his profound and tearful experience, can teach us a universe about the management of pain.

Pain is a three-dimensional phenomenon; it has an x, y, and z axis. It has height, width, and depth. Let us begin with an analysis of the heights to which pain can rise.

Pain runs the gamut from the inevitable, such as old age and death on the one end, to the avoidable, such as injustice and tooth decay on the other. For each of these categories philosophy has a different response.

Pain that is avoidable today, such as paralysis from polio, was a threat to all children just a few years ago. There is thus a category of totally unnecessary pain.

There is also the category of pain, such as cancer, against which the rational person struggles by enlisting all will and intelligence. Philosophy can help by giving us the *will* to fight and by showing us that in this struggle we can find our destiny and the meaning of life.

Finally, there is the pain that is truly and forever inevitable. It is the pain suffered by the most successful and the happiest of people. That is the pain of human mortality, which means death and frustration. It is also the pain of human freedom, which means anguish and guilt.

An existential philosophy addresses itself to this category of pain by pointing out what at first may appear paradoxical, even outrageous; *that we choose our limitations freely because we know that they create the best possible life and the supreme happiness for us.* To understand this point is to have found the secret of personal maturity and human authenticity.

In religion this insight is translated into the statement "God, who is infinite, chooses to be human, which means to be finite. In order to create Himself as a human being, God must limit His infinity. God chooses Himself to be human because He knows that it is better to be human and finite than infinite and divine." The myth of creation is the story of that insight.

Philosophy can help each individual to recover that choice in the structure of his own consciousness. Existentially-oriented therapy will help each person discover that he makes (and wants to make) that choice. This choice is at the root of all *unavoidable* individual human suffering.

This map of the height dimension of pain means little unless you integrate it into your daily existence. Make a short list of your problems. Then divide them into three groups: those that you can readily avoid, those against which you must struggle and might win, and those which you, like all human beings, must accept. In constructing your list remember that all three groups often overlap in what at first, before philosophical analysis, we call a single pain problem. Once your list is reasonably accurate and complete, develop a response and make a plan on how to deal with your pain.

Following is an example of Pain Exercise I, taken from the journal of Roland, a thirty-two-year-old electrical engineer, married with two children.

A blank is included for your own use.

Name: *Roland B.*

Pain Exercise I. The Spectrum of Pain.

A.   List several troublesome pains in your life.
   (1) *Too many colds.*
   (2) *Constant car trouble.*
   (3) *Hate the smog.*
   (4) *Job is good but not meaning-giving.*
   (5) *Getting older without adequate achievement.*
   (6) *I have conflicts about mother, who should be placed in some kind of a home. I worry about the money and I am afraid she will move in with us.*

(7) *I am an outward success but inside me I am depressed and confused.*

(8) *I am afraid of being mugged.*

B. *ANALYSIS.* Reorganize the above pains into the following three groups (keep in mind that each pain is composite), explain your thinking and offer solutions.

(1) Pains that I can easily avoid:

Colds and car trouble can be helped with better planning and more intelligent living (regular hours, healthier foods). I can afford a better car and I think I will buy one. I have been too lazy.

Mugging. I can avoid dangerous times and places, even though I would be restricted. I can get better locks for the house.

(2) Pains against which I can struggle:

Smog. I can try to earn more and move out of the area. I can look for a job where the air is clean. I can try to persuade my wife, who likes it here, to move.

I can use my skills to help fight air pollution. In fact, I have wanted for some time now to join an activist group in the war against pollution. If I make a commitment for social involvement some of my guilt will be dissipated. Such work will give me meaning.

Job. I can look for ways to improve my job. In fact, some of us at the laboratory are getting together on a regular basis to see how we can humanize our jobs more. I could be really courageous and look for a second career that may give me greater meaning. I think I would like to go into medicine. On second thought, I think I'll make a proposal to Dr. G, the lab general manager, about practical ways to humanize the job. I have some constructive ideas. In fact, I'll write them up and submit it as an article for publication in one of the trade journals.

(3) Pains that I cannot avoid:

Mother's oncoming death.

> *My inner sense of depression about the meaningless of life.*
> *My anxiety of getting old without achieving anything.*
> *I think I need philosophy to deal with these problems.*

Name:

Pain Exercise I. The Spectrum of Pain.

A. List several troublesome pains in your life.
    (1)
    (2)
    (3)
    (4)
    (5)
    (6)

B. *ANALYSIS.* Reorganize the above pains into the following three groups (keep in mind that each pain is composite), explain your thinking and offer solutions.
    (1) Pains that I can easily avoid:

    (2) Pains against which I can struggle:

(3) Pains that I cannot avoid:

On the basis of the avoidable-unavoidable classification of pain (what is called here the ladder or the height dimension), we can offer Roland the following simplified diagnosis.

The pains listed under B1 require for their amelioration little more than willpower and determination. Willpower results from understanding and exercising the freedom with which all of us are born. Roland must be helped to rediscover the freedom that defines his human nature. He can then use this knowledge to bring about the minor modifications listed under B1.

The pains listed under B2 may never be removed, although there is hope. Roland must resolve to fight. His answer is to be found in his protest. Roland is alienated, and the struggle against his depression is his answer, because it becomes his connection with the world. Also, the struggle is his meaning; it gives him something important and real to do. The struggle against pollution and against dehumanization on the job will help him recognize his worth: others need him. Finally, the humane causes will give him commitment; through them, he will express his responsibility to his fellow man. He will cease being an isolated individual and become a social being. Roland needs that challenge for the creation of his meaning.

He will find that, far from being threatened by redirecting his profession and his education, he will instead redirect his life from depression to joy.

But in order to deal with the pains that he lists under B3 — separation from mother, death, anxiety, and the general meaninglessness of existence — Roland needs philosophy. He has to learn to recognize that *being* Roland means being separated from his mother, facing ceaselessly the responsibility of creating his own meanings, and being eventually separated from life by death.

But he also must make the philosophic discovery that *he wants to be Roland* or at least that *he has chosen to be Roland.* If he now rechooses himself as Roland or rededicates himself to the choice already made, he will have achieved existential authenticity.

John, a thirty-five-year-old policeman who is in the process of making important personal and professional changes in his life, has the following entry in his journal. He describes well the agony involved in choosing to be himself.

Several days ago I experienced myself and my world in a way which is difficult to describe. My day was very rich. Not that it was pure pleasure or a day of rainbows. I had a major choice to make regarding a relationship which was painful for me. I had numerous experiences of my day but the most profound awareness was *my* awareness of the movement of my existence through each moment or event. I had a sense of homecoming or centeredness. That each event, each moment was ME. I could feel that each awareness (depression, elation, intellectualism, lying on the grass, anxiety) I had was mine and I owned them. It seemed as if it was MY world and my inwardness flowed from moment to moment. I felt truly alive. I experienced my aliveness and being as being projected out into the world. I was the locus of me or my projections. It was my world and I felt Godlike. I didn't feel I was God but rather that I was not the trees and windmill being blown by the wind but that *I was the wind.* The unbounded feeling of movement was very exciting. While sitting in class, studying in the library, driving to school, making a choice to leave a relationship, lying on the grass—all of these awarenesses were ME. I was the center of these experiences. I owned them.

Then something happened the next day. I awoke feeling a loss of me. I felt a profound sense of estrangement from myself. I was now being blown by the wind. My response was dread and anxiety in losing myself. I tried to recapture the day before—to reclaim me—to return to the center of myself and my world which I owned the day before. During my session with my therapist. I screamed in horror at

the loss of the sense of "being" and aliveness. As the painful session
continued I started to experience that my pain, dread and estrangement was ME. What I was the day before was then and me. And,
what I was in that session was NOW and also me. As I began to experience ownership of my dread and loss of my "being" I had a sense of
returning home, of centeredness, and of movement.

Looking back now, I feel that I experienced the "miracle of being"
and the horror of non-being, or non-aliveness and death. Perhaps
the profound impact, awe and bewilderment of being alive and a
sense of having touched God put me in touch with my resistance of
the death of myself as a totally alive human being.

11

The Depth of Pain

Every pain comes in layers. And each successive layer exposed in stripping pain down to its core tells us more about our nature as human beings. Pain leads to philosophic knowledge about the meaning of being a person. A tragic sense of life is prerequisite to understanding ourselves. We must prize this opportunity for self-knowledge, because it is only through pain that the essence of our humanity, our difference from the animals and from God can be fully understood and appreciated. Our happiness-oriented culture is an escape from the responsibility of understanding ourselves.

In existential personality theory, the *surface* layers of pain are called neurotic, pathological, or inauthentic. That is the pain which concerns physicians and therapists. It is the pain which results from illness and can be "cured" with drugs, surgery, and therapy. It is the pain which destroys the body and paralyzes the mind, truncates meaningful human relationships and limits effective interaction with the environment.

Deep layers of pain are philosophical, authentic, and existential. This pain is typically human, "incurable"; it is strength-giving and inspiring. The deepest layers of pain define the meaning of human existence.

The surface levels of pain—neurotic pains—are frequently second-order pains. They are pains about pains. Examples would be anxiety about anxiety, guilt about guilt, and the resentment of injustice.

The concept of layers of guilt can be clarified through an illustration. Gloria, a legal secretary, married for eleven years and childless, is tempted into an affair with one of her boss' clients. She feels guilty; in fact, she faces several layers of guilt. Her deepest level of guilt is the conflict between unfulfilled possibilities (if she rejects the affair) and violation of a trusting relationship (her husband loves and trusts her). This conflict exists in the very nature of human beings and the social world into which we are born. She can be helped to gain strength and comfort from the insight that her deepest layer of guilt is as much part of her humanity as is the circulation of her blood and her breathing.

A *medium* layer of guilt is learned. It is a social, tribal, or anthropological phenomenon rather than a philosophical one. Society has taught Gloria the powerful force of two conflicting claims: (1) love is good and must be sought and (2) adultery is a sin and must be avoided. Whichever way Gloria chooses— husband or affair—she will have violated a social canon and will thus feel guilt. That is the guilt of her superego, her conscience; it is the guilt arising from a violation of the internalized rule, the rule introjected by a foreign authority. This medium or social level of conflict is not to be confused with the deep or philosophical level discussed above. Medium or social guilt can be allayed only through a change in culture. Deep or philosophical guilt is embedded in the eternal nature of human existence.

Gloria experiences guilt while she believes "normal" and "healthy" people do not suffer from guilt feelings. She feels guilty, in the sense of feeling both inadequate and responsible for that inadequacy. Surface guilt comes from violating the demand of conformism. Gloria's surface guilt is her feeling that she "is different" or is not "keeping up with her friends." Surface guilt may also be the fear that she does not conform to her parents' wishes.

There are then at least three layers of guilt: philosophical, social, and psychological. Only the last two are subject to change: social guilt through cultural transformations and psychological guilt through psychotherapy. Philosophical guilt can only be understood and accepted; it cannot be changed. Whereas social and psychological guilt are damaging—they truncate the growth of the individual and must be overcome through therapy and social action — philosophical guilt can be illuminating, self-disclosing, and invigorating. Philosophical guilt puts man in touch with his essence and thereby gives him the strength to choose himself, to embrace himself and his destiny and thus to live fully.

Philosophy can show Gloria that the surface layers of guilt are based on ignorance. When philosophical wisdom is integrated into her life she can be free of needless pain, thus making room for a constructive use of philosophical pain. Surface pain hides the truth and debilitates the spirit, whereas the depth of pain is the challenge that makes life real and meaningful. Her unavoidable, and thus real, guilt is the conflict between two values: loyalty (to her husband) and love (in the affair). Conflict itself is an ultimate philosophic reality about human beings because each of these incompatible values is an essential truth about human existence. When Gloria recognized that her guilt was the full depth of her human situation, she gained strength and inspiration for the challenge. She overcame the suspicion that she was inferior and had a problem that she could not resolve. In fact, meeting this challenge — more than choosing between being loyal or being loving — was what eventually gave joy and meaning to her life. After one year of confronting the challenge of her existential conflict, Gloria left her husband *and* the affair. She ultimately entered into a new marriage on a far more mature basis than anything she had ever done up to that point in her life.

To inject these insights into real situations we again use Roland's journal. Roland is asked to analyze his pains and determine what portion of them is philosophic and what is not (and thus based on philosophic ignorance and lack of self-disclosure). Use Roland's answers as guidelines to develop your own answers for Pain Exercise II. Use the blank provided on page 147.

How can deep philosophical pain be integrated into life? How can life be better because of pain based on the philosophical nature of humankind?

Name: *Roland B.*

Pain Exercise II. The Layers of Pain.

A. Describe what you believe to be the ontological, authentic, existential or philosophic layer of the pains that you examined in Exercise I. List at least two elements of that layer.

My life has no meaning because life in general has no meaning. I can and must give and assign meanings to my life. I see that and it is clear to me that I have the free will to do it.

B. What do you propose to do to manage the pain on a philosophical level?

I must and can decide what really is important to me in life. I must have the courage to realize that I have pursued false gods for most of three decades. I become strong as I permit myself to feel the grief of stupidly having thrown away life's most precious values for so many years. I hurt, but the hurt makes me strong—as long as I can feel it. It is an almost physical sensation in my chest. I can imagine how superstitious people believe God or a spirit has entered them and given them strength, or eternal life, or something like that.

Right now I feel free and have no difficulty in determining my real values. I want to love my wife and be loved by her. I want to love my two children and be loved by them. I want to be a good father to my Melissa and Kathy so they can be proud of me when they are grown women.

I also want to contribute to society through my electrical engineering profession. I genuinely want to improve the world and be appreciated for being of service. I guess I yearn for warm relationships with people rather than aloof connections with mathematical abstractions and with tapes and computers, lathes and solder.

I will be more affectionate with my family and more dedicated on my job. I will be more helpful and thoughtful towards the men who work for me.

Pain Exercise II. The Layers of Pain.

A. Describe what you believe to be the ontological, authentic, existential or philosophic layer of the pains that you examined in Exercise I. List at least two elements of that layer.

B. What do you propose to do to manage the pain on a philosophical level?

Negation is the essence of pain. What does that mean?* Take any experience of pain whatever—moral, physical, or emotional—and reduce it to its general and final meaning. You will find that in all pain the individual ego discovers that the world says *no* to it; pain is the *no* of the world. Pain is the experience of the boundaries that the world imposes on people. The problem of pain thus becomes the problem of managing humanity's finiteness. And this is an important conclusion.

You can now rephrase for yourself the problem of pain. Your life is surrounded by walls, barriers, boundaries, abso-

---

*Rather than *pain* or *suffering* we should use the philosophical term *negation* to refer to painful experiences generally. The philosophy of religion has called our question the problem of evil. The book of Job in the *Old Testament* is devoted to this problem. The Bible asks, in effect, What does evil mean in the perspective of a world dominated by an infinitely good and all powerful God? Our philosophic question therefore becomes, "What is the meaning of negation? What does the negative in life tell us about the values of life? How can philosophy help us come to terms with the negative in life? How can we ever truthfully say that we choose negation from the infinite freedom of our inward consciousness?"

lute limits. How do you feel about the idea of limits in general? Do you feel like a prisoner who is held back, who is deprived of the real and the desirable world beyond? Or do you instead feel like an animal in a zoo, protected in your cage from the threats of the onrushing and unpredictable crowds? Are these boundaries like moats which keep you from climbing into the castle? Or are they instead more like mountains which you love to climb? Your answer to these questions is critical. If the idea of a limit is a prison, then the world is essentially evil. If, however, the idea of a limit represents to you a zone of protection or is for you an invigorating challenge, like climbing a mountain to achieve a spectacular view, then it is precisely these limits that give both reality and meaning to your life.

Let us assume your answer is the former and that your limits in life are so severe as to embitter you. Ask yourself if you can move your limits back far enough to change them from being frustrating to being challenging. We can symbolize this transformation by thinking of a heavy castle gate which imprisons you. By pushing on the gate, you can make it lean over to cover the moat and act as a bridge. What at first frustrated you now has been changed sufficiently—without being destroyed—to aid you in your movement toward freedom.

Ultimately, it is being finite that is intolerable. The person who affirms the glory of existence by saying *yes* to life must learn to manage this unacceptable condition. The first step in the management of negation is to recognize that pain is real. Our society conspires against that knowledge. We live in a pill-pushing and pill-popping society. A pill can dull the senses and stupefy the mind, but it cannot help human beings come to terms with the realities of negation. A pill hides the truth and makes the task of attaining philosophic insight just that much more arduous.

The discovery of negation is the discovery of our human essence. Each pain, each negation, uncovers its own unique human essence. Negation, in disclosing our human essence, shows to us the phenomena of (1) *constitution* (A3 on the Master Table), (2) The *Other* (C9 and C10 on the Master Table), and (3) *the desirability of finitude* (C1, C2, and C14). In a larger sense, the existence of negation makes possible growth (C13) and life itself (C8).

Constitution means that I, as a free and responsible agent, create, organize, produce, or bring about a particular way of perceiving reality. Specifically, constitution of the *Other* means that I assume responsibility for creating a world for myself in which an independent Other is the central feature. Constitution of *finitude* means that I assume full, deliberate, free, and creative responsibility for my own limits, my own finiteness. In short, I choose myself as finite. If I were God, I would, in my infinite wisdom, relinquish my infinity and voluntarily limit myself as a human being. That is the meaning of the constitution of finitude. Thus, constitution requires negation, the existence of the Other implies negation, and the choice of finitude is an act of negation. Therefore, all the phenomena that are the essence of consciousness — constitution, the Other, and finitude — contain the element of pain in their being.

For anything to exist and to be known, its opposite is required. The Latin word *existere* means, literally "to stand out"; to exist is for something to come into being and then to call attention to itself by being different from its background. Contrast is needed for existence, experience, and perception. Light is not something perceived in itself: It is manifested to the experiencing organism only after it has met its Other and has been reflected by it. Neither the concept nor the experience of light or day can exist except as they are brought into relief through a background of shadow and night. If night did not exist, we would have to invent it and preserve it in our imagination to give meaning to the concept of daylight. In the process of creating, constructing, or "constituting" the meaning of light, we automatically and inevitably bring about the idea of night, its Other. As with the magnet used to illustrate the concept of consciousness, or with electrical phenomena, a positive charge brings about its opposite, a negative charge. The negative charge is its Other, and the existence of the positive charge has no meaning and no reality without the existence of its Other.

Is that situation bad? Not at all. If we love music we do not denigrate silences because they momentarily rob us of sound. Every listener recalls the effective pause in the Hallelujah Chorus of Handel's *Messiah,* in which the climactic notes are introduced by a conspicuous period of silence.

Furthermore, life is a meaningful concept only because of the idea of death. Again in this case we would have to invent our death in order to be aware of the fact that we are alive. Ask yourself, in full honesty, this question: If there were no death, real or imagined, would the statement "I am alive" have any meaning whatever? If life itself is our greatest value, would we not have to invent death to be conscious of life?

This insight, that opposites create, is compressed in the very meaning of the word *definition.* To define means to delimit, to set boundaries, because to bring out the meaning of a concept is to show its borders, to indicate what it is *not.*

In a similar vein we can say that joy exists as a meaningful idea only because there also is suffering. The joy-suffering contrast is experienced vividly upon recovering from an illness. It is also found in the vertigo that follows hyperventilation. When the patient experiences some relief from the agonies of vertigo he slips into brief moments of euphoria.

Let us now move from our specific analysis of constitution to a consideration of the Other. The only answer to loneliness and aloneness is the discovery that there exists another — person, animal, or natural object — in this world. The Other is our roots. In our society, which pays lip service to mobility and independence, not enough attention is given to the feelings of rootedness and the need for a home. Even enemies are preferable to no one at all, a fact seen in the relationships that sometimes develop between prisoner and guard or criminal and victim. The Other is a necessary aspect of consciousness. The Other, by its nature, *opposes* the subject of consciousness. Sometimes this opposition is called hate, sometimes love. But always it is the Other. The Other can be a person or nature. Every experience in which we feel real, substantial, joyous, and alive is an experience in which we have discovered the reality of the Other; we have discovered that we are not alone in this world. Nature is real, not an illusion. People are real, not illusory. The world is real, and not a dream. If we were truly alone, like God before Creation, we indeed would have to invent the Other in order to feel real, to understand that we exist and to overcome our loneliness. Here we see the deep meaning of the myth of Creation: God creates Nature as His Other; thus the second root of pain lies in its Otherness. And Otherness is beautiful.

We want negation; we choose it and assume full responsibility for it; negation is an aspect of humanity's supreme good.

It is cruel and insensitive, in fact even false, to tell someone who suffers deeply that he really *wants* the suffering and that the pain is really for the best. This is reminiscent of an older age in which pain, like poverty, was believed to be the result of moral depravity. The value I speak of here is different.

Waldo is an extremely talented twenty-three-year-old violinist. He has positions in several leading orchestras in the western United States, practices a major part of the time, and has been able to make unusual coaching arrangements with a couple of world-famous musicians. Recently, Waldo was offered a contract to play both the Beethoven and the Tchaikovsky violin concerti in several solo performances with a top East Coast orchestra. Taping sessions for a major record company were also included in the contract. It was the opportunity of his lifetime. He commuted to rehearsals, which meant weekly flights across the U.S. The first rehearsals were unexpectedly successful. Waldo had never played better in his life. The weekly flights were no problem, because he had flown from earliest childhood and even had a pilot's license. Although Waldo's family was from San Francisco, he had spent many years in Paris and also went to school in Rome, making frequent transatlantic flights. It came therefore as a disturbing surprise to Waldo that from the time of the signing of his contract as soloist he began to develop serious bouts of airsickness. As soon as he entered the airplane he would panic—as if he had suddenly developed claustrophobia. Once in the air, he became dizzy, nauseous, and blacked out for short periods of time. Flying, which all his life had been easy and fun for Waldo, now, at the height of his career and when he most depended on it, became an intolerable ordeal.

The following, in Waldo's own journal, is his record of how he attempted to deal philosophically with this catastrophic development.

I feel like total hell. I've never played better. I've never had a better opportunity to make it big. I am about to enter the big-league concert and recording career. I am on the threshold to greatness and I am too weak to take it! I feel fine and buoyant but I'm so sick on the plane that I would rather die than go on.

God dammit! I am going to decide to cope with this situation! "I choose to cope! I choose to cope!" That's what Dr. Koestenbaum used to say.* This choice is rational only; it is abstract. In truth, I don't want to cope. I've lost heart. But I do make the choice not to cope, to black out. I make it feebly. I will follow the instructions for this journal.

I am sick when I am most successful. I am myself stopping myself at the height of my career. I am suffering from what Dr. Koestenbaum calls the "hubris-nemesis syndrome." My consciousness is introducing negation into itself.

I get sick when I am up high. The height of the airplane is like the apex of my career, my playing. I stop myself at the height. My consciousness negates itself automatically. It is the collective unconscious, the ancient myth of man who is being punished for the arrogance of his success.

I can sense how self-negation is built into the structure of consciousness itself. "Each action produces an equal reaction." The more successful my consciousness is the more it puts on the brakes. Negation seems to resurface in myths, religion, philosophy, dreams and in the functioning of my body and psyche. Consciousness is like God, it cannot exist without its Other. My consciousness is soaring dangerously high, to God. It will lose itself if it continues to soar! My consciousness introduces the limits of its Otherness as if this were some ancient and deep wisdom.

I feel at this moment of my thinking that I am assuming responsi-

---

*C 8 on the Master Table.

bility for my airsickness! I feel euphoric. I seem at this very moment to be integrating my airsickness into my total life and a weight is lifted! But I fear that even this success is hubris and will not be permitted. It does give me a headache! I am condemned to fail even in the understanding of my failure. O God, I punish myself for my success and then I punish myself all over again for *understanding* that I punish myself for my success!

My airsickness is the Otherness that is thrown as limit into the face of my soaring ego, my flying consciousness. But it is true that my airsickness, if perceived in its philosophic truth, gives me a sense of being a concrete ego. I feel like a real self and a strong consciousness. For God's sake, let me admit once and for all that *I want to feel like hell! It is good for me to feel like hell! I want to place obstacles in the way of my violin! I love those obstacles! Those brakes are good!* My neck bulges and I feel like screaming!

Waldo has assumed free and full personal responsibility for the negation that exists so disturbingly in his life. He says he places it there, and he does so because he wants to. He knows that it is the mature functioning of consciousness that is involved. He knows that he is in touch with the structure of his pure consciousness, with the intentionality of being. His life is perceived by him to be an expression of the phenomenon of constitution itself. He senses with powerful directness how his consciousness is constituting Otherness and finitude in his life. And if he has any philosophic understanding at all, he would never have it otherwise.

His next step is to translate his philosophical discovery — that airsickness is his way of limiting the infinity of his consciousness for the sake of feeling *real* — more humanistically into his present life situation. The philosophical insight has appeared to him in an "impractical" way. The insight does what it says. It says, "you need negation" and it *gives* him that negation by making his life difficult. The insight itself is thus an instance of further negation. The insight in turn becomes the challenge. It is instructive to follow Waldo's journal — next is an entry written two months later — and his attempt to integrate the pain into a more mature life and better musicianship for him. His words express how suffering translates itself into meaning, pain into joy, whenever we are in touch with the philosophic roots of negation.

I have discovered two ways of philosophically integrating my airsickness with my commitment to the violin. I have learned how to fight fate with my music; but I have also learned how to flow, in complete passivity, with life. As a result my playing has developed a virtuosity it did not have before. The conductor, Maestro G____, told me my playing had become sweet and mellow without losing the brilliance for which I had been known. He told me I played like a much older and more experienced musician than I was. Mr. D_____ of the _____newspaper, told me the "authority" of my playing was that of a master. I now possessed maturity in addition to technical virtuosity.

My playing is not just an attack on frustration or obstacles. My fight is steep, like a parabolic curve. The more I fight the tougher the fight gets. I am always just a bit ahead of myself. Man, am I moving fast!

I let myself go with the stream of the conflict between the violin and the airsickness. I no longer try to fight *against* airsickness or *for* the violin.* I look at this conflict before me in my life, so intimate and threatening earlier, like a Shakespearean tragedy. I almost enjoy watching the ridiculous struggle between my soaring success, which recalls the high notes on the E-string, and my nonsensical obstacle, like a string which nightmarishly breaks again and again. I feel I float weightless and silent on a wave. The gates of my unconscious must be open and the contents freely released. My playing is easy. My nausea does not worry me. I laugh at it. It has changed my playing. I am no longer recognized as the same violinist. I move with the stream of the conflict the way a seagull floats on the waves of the ocean or a trout facing upstream is suspended completely still against the clear waters of a rushing stream. I have never felt this much at ease in my life before.

There is another thing. I play that conflict in my concerts. I rebel against it; I love it; I observe it; I overlook it. If you ask today, "What do you say with your playing?" my answer is "I celebrate the reality of

---

*C 14 on the Master Table.

consciousness by choosing its opposition. I give effect and lots of feeling to an abstract philosophical truth!"

The history of consciousness has once more reaffirmed itself, and this time in the life of Waldo. By choosing to cope, he has been able to assume responsibility for his pain and to experience it in that aspect which is truly self-willed. The self-willed aspect of pain appeared to him the moment he recognized the universal philosophical ingredient underlying his rather particularized problem.

A recording of one of Waldo's performances is among my most cherished possessions. Remember:

1. The only pain that concerns philosophy is the pain that is inevitable.

2. Try choosing to be what or who you already are. Try really to accept yourself for what you are. You will feel tremendous relief.

3. Your pains and frustrations will give depth and meaning to your life, if you can only learn how to *protest* vigorously against them.*

4. A tragic sense of life is the beginning of self-knowledge.

5. Negation in your life simply means you know you are real.

6. Negation in your life means you know you are never alone.

7. Negation in your life means you have put on your brakes to slow down in order to enjoy your trip.

---

*Protest, through the mechanism of no-saying, makes us conscious of the Other. As a result we experience the reality of our concrete individual existence.

12

The Types of Pain

Although there is overlap, different kinds of pain disclose different aspects of human reality. Understanding what each individual pain can reveal to us about the philosophical essence of humanity is helpful in guiding each of us to the necessary existential management of pain. For example, a person who suffers deeply from guilt would need to approach his program for philosophical self-disclosure differently from one whose principal problem was frustration. Whereas guilt may reveal the eternal freedom of human beings, frustration may reveal the inevitable as well as desirable reality of the Other. Reference to your individual profile derived from the pain test is useful here.

The following are guidelines only, since a particular negative word does not always designate the same painful experience and even the same experience does not always yield predictable material.

Anxiety and dread represent some of the most important negative philosophical experiences. Existentialism has long held that anxiety reveals deep truths to us, truths not available through other means, such as the senses or scientific measurements. Furthermore, the truths thus revealed answer the questions associated with our needs for meaning, authenticity, and human fulfillment.

This cluster of negative experiences called anxiety and dread can be evoked by such words as *desperate, agitated, afraid, awful, terrified, panicky, shaky, separated, lost, rejected, homeless,* and *unloved.*

Anxiety and *dread* are central to existential philosophy because they disclose the region of pure consciousness in human experience. This is the pure zone of subjectivity, the observer never observed, the silent solitary center. In short, anxiety and dread disclose the nature of consciousness. And that is quite a discovery! Consciousness has been denied, ignored, and explained away. Anxiety reestablishes the reality of consciousness; it provides an experience which gives us direct access to the most important and central phenomenon of human existence: consciousness. Philosophically understood then, anxiety is no longer a disease which embarrasses us and which must therefore be tranquilized.

Consciousness can also be understood intellectually. The philosopher René Descartes invented and applied the method of systematic and universal doubt. He accepted nothing that could be doubted. And because everything is subject to doubt, he would have become a skeptic except for one basic fact: The existence itself of consciousness cannot be doubted. It is consciousness that does the doubting. First consciousness is needed so that doubt can then exist. There is something eternal about the mystery that is subjective and inward consciousness. Descartes thus demonstrated the necessary existence of the region of pure subjective consciousness. Doubt is the intellectual equivalent of what the emotions call anxiety. In other words, the *emotion* of anxiety reveals experientially what the *concept* of doubt demonstrates intellectually—namely, the indestructibility of consciousness, and the fact that its existence is logically necessary. This is one of the central discoveries of humankind.

How, specifically, does anxiety reveal? Fear of loss is concern for a specific object. In that fear, the object is lost but the rest of the world remains; replacements are therefore possible. But anxiety is different; it is, as Heidegger has pointed out, the fear that the world itself will be lost. Anxiety is the dread that nothing remains, not even the world. Nothing remains but the *consciousness of total nothingness*. The concept of nothingness

is needed in existentialism to describe and evoke the phenomenon of pure and eternal consciousness. It is a poetic metaphor; it is an important image.

The concept in psychology that comes closest to this philosophical emotion of anxiety about nothingness is "separation
anxiety." To a small child, the mother is the whole world.
Remove the mother, and to the poor child all that remains in
this world is its own pure consciousness—reaching, reaching
and reaching, and nothing else! The object of the reaching—
in fact, all objects—have gone. The light of the child's consciousness is in search of an object that will reflect it. There is
no object, because the mother is gone. There is only empty
space. As a result, there is no luminosity at all to the child's
world; only utter darkness, complete nothingness. That is the
experience of dread, despair, and of ultimate anxiety. But it is
also the experience of pure consciousness, for what remains
when the whole world of objects has been erased is the absolute
and empty reaching consciousness. Separation anxiety is like
the ray of pure light that has lost all objects to illuminate. It is
an arrow, pointing forever at nothing at all. In separation
anxiety the ego is finally forced to look only upon itself, to see
itself as it is, to comprehend its mysterious and saintly nature.
Therefore, dread is, strictly speaking, not an emotion at all; it
is not the fear of an object. Dread is a philosophical event.
Dread is a philosophical revelation. Dread is the nakedness of
consciousness; its dress, which is the object, has been stripped
away.

Naked consciousness, pure awareness, and objectless perception are unique experiences, alternately dreadful and euphoric. They are dreadful because the world is gone; but they
are also euphoric, because consciousness remains—with all its
extraordinary attributes of eternity,* timelessness, indestructibility, and the power of spontaneous and free creation.

Existential philosophy transforms anxiety from an emotion,
a mere disease, to a complex event containing within it a dia-

---

*Pure consciousness has some of the characteristics of God. This point is
developed in Chapters 18 and 19 of my book *The Vitality of Death* and in *Is
There an Answer to Death?*

mond core of priceless insight. And, paradoxical though it seems, in philosophy, anxiety can lead to true peace of mind.

Authentic versus Neurotic Anxiety

The anxiety that discloses philosophic truths is healthy and authentic. Neurotic anxiety hides and distorts, whereas authentic anxiety discloses the nature of pure consciousness, neurotic anxiety is often an expression of alienation. When the subjective and objective aspects of the field of consciousness are intentionally related,* then there is a sense of peace, grace, and ease. This is my definition of health and authenticity. Under these circumstances, the anxiety level is very low. However, if that continuity of consciousness with its world is broken, then life is experienced as burdensome and troubled; it becomes artificial and must be held together with raw willpower. Life is then bereft of meaning, for the artificial values upheld and constructions maintained are in constant threat of collapse. The relaxed sense of being natural and thus supported by the harmony between persons and world is gone. The willpower that holds life together is experienced as anxiety about the loss of truth and meaning. It is a most uncomfortable way to live, and yet it is common. This is one aspect of neurotic anxiety. There is another way to describe the break of continuity in consciousness, a break that is called alienation.

Our bodily life occurs in the empirical realm, in the ego, the body, the personality, and the emotions. These terms represent the objective pole of the field of consciousness. If our bodily existence has no access to the realm of pure, subjective consciousness—then there can *be* no field on consciousness and no growth. That is the situation in neurotic anxiety.

A person who is neurotically anxious because the two poles of his field of consciousness are alienated from each other has a "constipated" or a withholding character structure; he does not transcend himself, emerge, or move. He has no time and

---

*See the chapter on *Metaphors for Consciousness.*

no growth in his life. Such a person "kills" himself and others, in that he squelches the connection between the inner and outer worlds. He kills authenticity in himself and is thus incapable of responding to it in others. If he is a parent, he will squelch his children. Such a person deadens himself and those dependent on him by jailing and frustrating himself and others. He is unresponsive and, in general, unloving. This person is not in touch with his feelings or his body. He fails himself in love and sex. The themes on the Master Table concerned specifically with anxiety are C1 and C2.

Another important existential emotion is guilt. The existential meaning of guilt can be evoked by such adjectives as *worthless, destroyed, unjust, unfair, shameful,* and *ashamed.* The structure disclosed by the worldly emotion of guilt is freedom. In other words, the experience of guilt tells us that freedom is the meaning of human existence, an integral aspect of the consciousness that I am. Guilt is the experience that I could have acted otherwise. Guilt therefore accompanies all of our choices, because to the extent that the options on which my decisions are based were real I could have meaningfully decided otherwise than I did. The gut realization of this fact of freedom is the experience of guilt. Guilt, to the degree that it reveals my freedom to me, can thus be a source of extraordinary strength and authenticity, for freedom is the experience of my creative powers and of my life's energy.

Of what practical use is this revelation about my freedom? To know that guilt is freedom is to change weakness into strength, worry into self-confidence, and failure into success. To understand that guilt is proof of freedom is to move from paralysis to action, from being destroyed to being creative. In short, to find freedom in guilt is to overcome the paralysis of neurotic guilt and to experience the creative power of existential guilt.

Words that evoke the philosophical meaning of physical pain are obvious expressions like *hunger, thirst, illness, headache, toothache, cramps, nausea.*

In terms of the existential theory developed here, physical pain reveals the inner structure of the mysterious philosophical relationship that we (our consciousness) have to our body (our ego). According to the field-of-consciousness theory, when we are in the act of perceiving our own bodies, then the ego is the subject and our body becomes an object to that ego. It is at this time of reflection that the details of our attachment to our bodies become visible. Pain is the experience of holding on to that attachment when the logic of the situation would be to let go. Medical tests, operations, dental work, injuries, and disease show us the dominion of the body over our spirits. We can reverse this relationship and view it from the inside of our consciousness, rather than from the outside of our body as does the medical practitioner.

How does it feel to be in the agony of pain? The body obtrudes itself on our consciousness. The body is so close to us that we have lost control over it. We certainly have lost the distance that spells sanity to us (principles A2 and C3 of the Master Table). We can therefore no longer enlist the help of the body to move around in the world. Think of an old-fashioned horse buggy. The driver controls the energy of his horses. The distance from him to the horses is needed for control. The experience of pain corresponds to the loss of that distance—the driver is on top of the horses or he is stampeded by them. Pain is also the horses going wild, ripping loose from the wagon, and dragging the driver with them. Then the pain is in holding on.

The pain will stop if the driver releases the reins. But so will the connection of consciousness and body, of subject and object poles in the field of consciousness. We cannot leave the body, of subject and object poles in the field of consciousness. We cannot leave the body, because most of us have been taught that this means death and that death is evil. The pain is our holding on to our identification with the body. It is also our holding on to the organization which we have imposed upon it for the sake of the practical and individualized aspects of our life. When I am in pain I cannot walk, drive, work, cook, or travel. The direction of authentic consciousness, which in health moves from ego to body, has now been reversed or severed altogether.

In the agony of pain it makes sense to let go of the body—to relinquish it, to abandon it, to separate from it. We call this state death, anesthesia, or unconsciousness. But we hold on to the body, literally, "for dear life." The exploration of physical pain discloses to us the answer to the important philosophical problem of the relation between the body and consciousness.

How can inward descriptions of the consciousness of pain aid in managing pain? The answers are found in *withdrawal* and *perspective*. Withdrawal means retreating into the space of consciousness away from the identification with the body. Withdrawal as a solution to the problem of pain may lead in selected cases to mild forms of self-hypnosis. Concentrate on "looking at" the pain rather than "being" the pain. Train yourself to be the observer of your pain. Do not identify yourself with the pain. Such dissociation cannot, however, be performed with fine discrimination for painful experiences only. It leads to indiscriminate dissociation not only from the pain but also from all actions and any pleasures.

For example, suppose you have an injured right foot. Think of the foot with its pain as being as far away from your center as possible. It helps if you imagine it to be the foot of someone else. The greater the experienced distance from your conscious center to the location of the pain, the more bearable the pain will be. But as you withdraw successfully, you will find that two things happen. You become generally inactive. If your foot is injured, withdrawal from the pain means also that you will do nothing to help yourself. To help yourself means deliberate action and body control. Philosophical withdrawal, on the other hand, means to give up that control. Furthermore, withdrawal means to relinquish our usual value system. Withdrawal means to give up the value of health and even of life itself. It means adopting an I-don't-care attitude about everything. Philosophic withdrawal therefore, carries a steep price, and should be used, like any anesthetic, with great caution.

Let us now turn to the perspective that is achieved by recognizing through pain the mind-body relationship. Pain may not be allayed by being understood. But the meaning of life is grasped by that understanding. And once we are familiar with the larger designs of human existence, the threat of dying and the ruin of ordinary social values has been conquered. Philosophy makes us free. And that freedom gives us the sense to live splendidly with whatever objective realities are in our power.

The experience of tragedy leads to an understanding of what I call the paradoxical, dialectical, polar, or intentional, character of consciousness. It is this character of consciousness—built into the very nature of reality itself—that surfaces in the emotional life of humanity as the experience of tragedy. Tragedy has always held a peculiar attraction for us. As an art form, it has been called "deep philosophy." The reason is that tragedy can reflect what is most real in being, the nature of consciousness itself.

The sense of tragedy is evoked by such words as *contradiction, paradox, sad, indecision, conflict, irresolvable, ambivalent, ambiguous.* In tragedy—traditionally the highest art form—the intrinsic ambivalence of the ego-world, subject-object interaction is experienced strongly and directly. Tragedy leads to tears—not tears of mere frustration and anger, but tears of insight and elevation, of depth and resolution. As is true of physical pain, the strength and inspiration found in tragedy does not come from a resolution of the conflict or ambivalence that it represents. Instead, tragedy opens windows to the truth about man—a truth, compressed in theme C14 of the Master Table, which transforms conflict from a debilitating problem to an invigorating challenge.

In some respects, tragedy is like a good marriage. To *resolve* a marital conflict is to *separate,* that is, to side with either husband or wife. To experience the oscillating conflict or the polar contrast as being the reality of the encounter between two human beings is to perceive the marriage as a success and as a higher level of human development than the unchallenged single status.

Tragedy is found in the unending *paradox* of wealth and poverty, peace and war, suffering and joy, justice and injustice, love and hate, success and failure, health and illness. These opposites have always existed and have puzzled suffering mankind. They will continue to plague us, for polarity is a name for the vibrancy of life itself. A nonpolar consciousness is no consciousness at all.

It is important to bring an element of reality and experience into this paradox. We can contrast two products of human consciousness, two consequences of human decisions. There has been and always will be the lowest evil side by side with the highest good. It is the contrast that gives rise to the sense of tragedy. A newspaper story reports,*

BABY SURVIVES FOUR DAYS ALONE

An 18-month-old baby lay four days in her crib without food or water while the body of her murdered mother lay on the floor a few feet away.

Authorities are looking for the baby's father, an AWOL soldier from nearby Fort Ord.

The baby was severely dehydrated, and her kidneys were not functioning.

She was taken to Ft. Ord Hospital and transferred to Letterman General Hospital in San Francisco. She was still being fed intravenously today but was in good condition.

The discovery was made Wednesday night by the apartment managers and sheriff's deputies.

"If we had found her (the baby) Thursday morning, we would have had two deaths," said the Monterey County Det. Sgt. _____.

He said she could not have lived another 12 hours.

The baby's 19-year-old mother was found on the floor of the bedroom in the apartment.

The baby apparently had been heard crying, but because there are several babies in the complex it could not be determined from which apartment the crying was coming.

The AWOL soldier's company commander had called at the home several times since Saturday in an attempt to get him to return to the base. He got no response to his knocks.

The last time the officer came to the apartment was Monday. He heard no sounds that day for the baby apparently had ceased crying by then.

The child's mother had been hit on the head with a blunt instru-

---

*San Jose News, Friday, June 30, 1972, page 2. Reprinted by permission.

ment, but it was not know immediately whether that was the cause of
death because the body had begun to decompose.

The same world that produced the action of that husband-
father also produced Ernesto Cardenal, who had the inspiration to write

All things love each other. All nature is oriented toward a *thou*. All
beings that are alive are in communion with each other. . . .
     All nature is in close touch and interwoven. All nature is in con-
stant embrace. The wind which caresses me and the sun which kisses
me, the air which I inhale, and the fish which swims in the water, the
distant star and I who behold it: we are all in closest touch with one
another. What we call the empty interstellar spaces are molded by
the same matter that informs the stars, even though in a tenuous and
rarefied way. The stars are but condensed forms of interstellar matter, and the entire universe is like one single immense star; and we all
participate in this universe in one and the same rhythm—the rhythm
of that universal gravity which accounts for the cohesion of an otherwise chaotic matter, a cohesion which joins the molecules together
and causes certain particles of matter to unite at a definite place of
the universe and which makes the stars what they are. And this unify-
ing force is the rhythm of love.
     Though we are all in close contact, we are all incomplete. This in-
complete nature of ours strives unceasingly for greater perfection,
and this striving we call evolution. The most perfect being in nature
is man. And yet man, too, is incomplete; he, too, is imperfect and
he, too, tends toward a *Thou:* he tends toward God. And when man
loves God, he loves Him with the same ardent desire that animates all
nature; he loves Him with the groaning of all creatures, with the immense perennial desire of the entire process of evolution. All creation
sighs with us, as St. Paul says, in the travails of birth, the travails of
the tremendous process of evolution.*

The authentic individual can live successfully in this world of
unconscionable paradox and can find his meaning, his true

---

*To Live Is to Love, trans. Kurt Reinhardt (New York: Herder and
Herder, 1972); pp. 21-22.

challenge, in that paradox: Success means that life's struggle is
set; it is struggle against the evil side of the paradox. We will
die in the struggle, but we will have sanctified life in the process.

The management of tragedy is to descend from tragedy
about tragedy (second-order tragedy) to simple and pure
tragedy. Real tragedy makes man serious and purposeful. It
makes him strong, gives him a proper sense of values and the
capacity to make any life a noble one. Second-order tragedy is
the nagging complaint about the existence of real tragedy; it is
the weak complaining about the strong; it is the weak having
contempt for the fulfilled. The authentic individual *wants* the
intentionality of consciousness reflected in his world. He *wants*
the movement of ambiguity. It is from the oscillation between
subject and object that authentic love is born, because love is
an eternally unresolved relationship between two incompatible
and fully joined poles.

The Bible dreams about the end of paradox.

The lion will live with the lamb, and the panther will lie down with
the kid, calf and lion cub will feed together, and a little boy will lead
them. The cow and the bear will make friends, and their young will
lie down together. The lion will eat straw like the ox, the infant will
play over the cobra's hole, and the young child will put his hand into
the viper's lair.*

Does Isaiah mean the paradox should end? that conflict will
cease? that incompatible interests will be resolved or compro-
mised? No. When we read this beautiful passage from the Old
Testament we become sad, not joyous. Isaiah merely enhances
our sense of tragedy. He tells us that love is beautiful; in fact,
its beauty shines brightest when it becomes most painfully obvious to us that such bliss can never be. A living being that
loves and protects, but does not live off his surrounding nature, will die of starvation. Conflict in nature reflects the oscillating phenomenon that is consciousness. Without its bipolarity, consciousness is not.

---

*Isaiah 11:6-8.

Man has no recourse; he must reach the realization that conflict is contrast and that contrast is what he himself would spontaneously create if he were God. What if there is disaster in your own personal life? Natalie's husband is a violent alcoholic who brings down catastrophe on her and the children. Should the wife and children say to themselves "What beautiful tragedy? What inspiring destruction of life's most precious values?" Not at all! The problem itself comes from ignoring tragedy. Natalie has never integrated the meaning of tragedy into her life. She has consistently refused to live with ambiguity. Every aspect of life has had to have for her an unambiguous solution. Because it is only when she recognizes that ambiguity and conflict are inevitable that she can gather her wits about her and take decisive action. Medical treatment, hospitalization, separation, or divorce — in other words, resolution of the problem — would have been the result of the integration of tragedy. She then would be saying, in effect, "Life is tragic; that insight makes me strong. I can therefore take courageous and rational action."

Some people live with too much tragedy; others do not have enough. Both types are inauthentic. The authentic individual has in his life the optimum amount of tragedy. This means that whatever tragedy there may be in his life, much or little, is for him the best possible living metaphor or practical symbol for his consciousness. In this way, an individual assumes responsibility for his life and chooses to make it meaningful.

Depression reveals to me that I have made the decision to say *no* to life. Adjectives that evoke the meaning of depression are *worthless, suicidal, unspirited, weak, tired, sad, blue, low, purposeless, pointless, disinterested, unconcerned*. The discovery that one has said *no* to life, that one has chosen freely to deny the value of life itself, can come only to him who has the courage to feel himself into his depression, who can work through his grief. He must feel sadder than sad; he must experience the incredible emptiness that exists at the conscious center of his being. Most of us are terrified to confront that emptiness, because we feel we cannot bear its destructive power.

When a depressed individual comes close to reaching the nadir of his depression he is like a desert farmer drilling for a well in the dry soil. The deeper he drills the more discouraged he becomes. In the end he strikes water. He *must* strike water eventually because he is on top of an underground water table. Similarly, the depressed person is on top of his decision to say *no* to life, because the desolate emptiness is this very decision. If the self-disclosing individual drills deeply enough into his depression, he will strike the wellspring of that negative decision. He will discover and experience the free decision of continuously saying *no* to life. What then? Here is the important point: Once he is in touch with that decision, he has uncovered the freedom that can say *yes* to life as well as *no*. Freedom is not conditioned, not determined. Freedom means we can say either *yes* or *no* with equal facility. There is no reason or argument that points to either way. To say *yes* to life is to choose reason; then and only then do rational arguments become relevant. But they do not apply to the decision itself, because that reason-instituting decision has already been made and need not be made again. If we discover the freedom that in now saying *no* to life *we have also discovered the freedom that can say yes to life.* And this is the answer to depression. Depression will not disappear automatically; but we can *make* it disappear if we choose to do so. And only each individual ego can make that decision.

In other words, there exists no guarantee that once this freedom has been recovered, the individual will choose *yes* rather than *no* to life. There is no guarantee that life will automatically be chosen. Death (real or symbolic) can be chosen with equal ease, or with as much difficulty, as life. But if philosophy has an answer for the depressed individual and the suicidal person, it lies in the discovery that depression is a choice made with the same equipment and the same facility as is the joyous affirmation of life.

Depression thus reveals the dormant power for self-affirmation in all of us, and this uncovering is accomplished by revealing how in depression the power of self-denial is in use already.

He who has reached these depths of his being is ready to handle successfully almost any depression.

A related type of pain is the sense of meaninglessness. It discloses the empty truth about the realm of values. We search for absolute values but in fact we must create our own. The discovery that the question of the meaning of life has no firm answers brings on the despairing sense of meaninglessness. However, meaninglessness also shows to each human being that he has the power of self-definition. He can create meanings for himself; he can set up values for his life. And above all he can, if he so chooses, set these values up in conformity with the field-of-consciousness theory of humanity. He can choose "natural" values, values in harmony with the field-of-consciousness theory, even though he is free to choose any value system whatever.

The sense of meaninglessness is associated with words such as *discouraged, indifferent, ennui, valueless, empty, bored,* and *disinterested.*

Except for the sense of meaninglessness, an individual will never understand that he has the Godlike capacity to establish a meaning for himself in life and that, while using it may be a mystery, a life of healthy reality awaits him. In therapy, when a person is reborn or turns around to finally give his life meaning, he has reached the insight that in fact life is meaningless but for his own free and courageous choices.

Meaninglessness is the lack of a home; it is the expulsion from paradise, the fall of man. The question "What are my values?" echoes through the universe but is never answered by the universe. Answers are created by courageous freedoms. If we choose to be our bodies, if we choose to identify our meaning with our bodily nature, if our self-image is biological, then we can be deeply touched by these words from the naturalist John Muir:

Thousands of tired, nerve-shaken, overcivilized people are beginning to find out that going to the mountains is going home; that wildness is necessity; and that mountain parks and reservations are useful not only as fountains of timber and irrigating rivers, but as fountains of life. (1898)

This insight does not mean, however, that nature will *truly* be our meaning, fill the emptiness of our center. But it *does* mean that the real grief of our homelessness can be felt. Muir's perception of nature gives us a glimpse of the home we crave, of the home that we *might* have. It does not give us that home. But by taking us close, it makes the pain of our true homelessness — the meaninglessness of existence — grievously obvious.

Here is a corporate business executive's powerful statement about meaninglessness in his life, taken from his journal. He is describing his marriage, which to him is the symbol of meaninglessness in his life:

Act One: Setting — dismal first apartment.
Enter the brick-mason of anti-sex
wrong words — splat — "I didn't mean *that!*"
empty look — splat — "What are you staring at?"
frozen glare — splat — "Why are you laughing?"
Up goes the wall — splat — splat —
brick on brick — haphazardly laid —

Act Two: Eyes stop meeting, fingers stop reaching, kisses turn to cheek-brushes

Act Two and a Half: — Children — all great, all well.
Need two parents
Too proud to be less than two parents

Act Three: Conversation
Conversations are such fragile, fuzzy pups. Furry, damp-warm, blind.
Trembling thirstily for the suck-warm, nectar-laden breast — but equally in need of the long, learned linguistics of the mother-tongue.
Grateful for the sibling rivalry.
Somehow fed, groomed, growing. The maturing conversation comes into focus from a fuzzy *there* to a laser-sharp *here.*

Well. That may be conversation-between-friends, but for lovers—an ephemeral, oral-genital intercourse is more the poetry of this petting. And in so exalted a setting, the empty gambit, the hollow openers, uttered because one's partner will remain silent forever if *someone* does not, in desperation, say *something*—the false replies—make a mockery of the entire relationship. Egos crumble and the wall goes higher splat—splat.

Act Four: Realization that there was more sex and love in three pre-marital months than twenty-three post-marital years—how many *thousand* calm, silent mornings, warm afternoons, slightly inebriated evenings wasted? How does love go? Let me count the ways.

Act Five: Children are going and soon the little old world takes another spin around the sun and the primal torture of having to face each other again, as in Act One and Two!

This time the partner-players know the plot; this time—no children fill the silent slots.

Final Curtain: A two-dimensional pale screen of wind-washed dunes—movement without change. Is this the life—good enough for ordinary purposes?
Is this why I am here?
Hell, I'm still there and I'd say I can't get here from there.

When you feel life is meaningless because there is no love—as poignantly described above—the first authentic response is protest. In that case you are determined to rebel against that aspect of fate and that facet of your human nature which troubles you. The second authentic response to meaninglessness is to recognize in that sense of meaninglessness the opportunity to be what you want to be, to establish for yourself the kind of life-world that only you can create. The answer to the problem of meaninglessness for this executive is to find in his own life situation specific and revolutionary ways to protest the meaninglessness he so clearly perceives. Because he describes his problem in a dramatic form, the participation in plays—as writer, actor or producer-promoter—might be a start toward meaning. Another start toward meaning may be a serious commitment to a psychotherapeutic relationship.

Still a third solution may be to demand love from his wife now by persistent reasons and insistent feelings. A final possibility is to get busy searching for love elsewhere, if the days of protest and of therapy are over.

Loneliness—*aloneness, isolation, rejection, self-pity, alienation*—reveals the *uniqueness* of the ego. Loneliness, although painful, leads to the realization that I cannot be replaced. I do my own suffering; no one can do that for me. But I also do my own enjoying; no one can be euphoric for me. I do my own eating and my own excreting; no one can do that for me either. I am unique; I am me; I am an individual. When I feel alone I discover not only the weighty burden but also the uplifting glory of the fact that I am myself and not somebody else. The "I am" experience is the beginning of an authentic and a fulfilling existence.

If I dislike loneliness, I am ignorant about my human nature and have false expectations of life. Once I understand human nature, I recognize in my loneliness the high value of human existence: to be a unique individual. Once this is fully realized, being a unique individual is no longer a burden or a curse, nor a cause for self-pity. It means that my turn has come to play the game of life. And I have been waiting for that turn for a long time. I finally can live!

My loneliness tells me that I am special.

The negative experience of frustration is allied to the anger-hostility-aggression syndrome. The experience of frustration can include, in addition to *anger* and *aggression,* such feelings as *bitterness, disgust, cruelty, hate, annoyance, destruction.*

The disclosure opened up by frustration is the reality of the Other in life. Frustration can be turned into love if we recognize that behind it lurks, at least in part, the childish desire to be alone with a fantasy world, the inability to confront the reality of the Other in existence.

To the philosophically ignorant, confrontation with the Otherness of the world is a disaster. Happiness seems to mean the elimination of the world, with its undeniable resistance to

penetration. But the philosophically aware person understands that it is precisely the world's resistance which brings
about the sense of reality proper. The shift from a fantasy
world without resistance to a real world with insurmountable
opposition is the conversion from the child to the adult, from
the immature to the mature, from the dreamer to the realist,
and from the inauthentic to the authentic. No one has stated
the meaning of the Other better than Emily Dickinson when
she wrote

> Elysium is as far as to
> The very nearest room,
> If in that room a friend await . . . *

One major point remains in our discussion of the philosophic
reduction of pain. And that is a program for the philosophical
management of pain. To that point we now turn in the next
chapter. Remember:

1. Pain leads to truth.

2. *Anxiety and dread* disclose the existence and nature of
your pure consciousness.

3. *Guilt* reveals to you that you have used your freedom.

4. *Physical pain* tells you that you love your body.

5. *Tragedy* discloses to you the polarities and ambiguities of
life. They are but expressions of the natural polarity of your
field of consciousness.

6. *Depression* reveals to you that you are now using your
freedom to say *no* to life.

7. If you feel life is *meaningless* you are aware that you
choose your own values, your own nature, and your self-
definition.

8. Before you choose your values you must protest against
the lack of values.

9. Your *loneliness* informs you that you are unique. You are
not somebody else.

---

*From *The Complete Poems of Emily Dickinson,* ed. by Thomas H. John-
son. Reprinted by permission of Little, Brown and Co.

10. *Frustration* reveals to you that the world beyond your inward consciousness is real and is *there for you*.

13

Managing Pain

Mrs. Z voluntarily requested hospitalization in a San Francisco institution because she had escalating suicidal fantasies, including impulses to jump, hang herself, and slash her wrists. She was anxious that these impulses and fantasies might come true. Mrs. Z was twenty-three years old at the time. She was placed under psychiatric observation and eventually told a tragic story indeed.

Her husband had insisted that she have sexual intercourse with another man while he watched. He found her a partner and, after some resistance, Mrs. Z complied. The new relationship blossomed beyond what her husband had intended. One day while Mr. Z was at work, she and the man were in bed at the Z residence. Mrs. Z's three-year-old boy, Douglas, wandered out of his room and into the backyard. She did not hear him because the door to her bedroom was locked. Douglas fell into the pool and drowned.

That was three months before Mrs. Z's voluntary admission to the hospital for fear of attempting suicide. During that three-month period Mrs. Z suffered periods of severe depression and ferocious anxiety.

Mrs. Z received philosophically-oriented therapy—that is, she went through an intensive existential analysis—and following is an outline of the process. It is a summary of the existential elements of long-term therapy.

Mrs. Z had a problem that meets two criteria for existential therapy: Her problem was a genuine paradox, an authentic conflict. There was (1) *no solution* and *(2)* its *agony* was unbearable. The conflict was between life and death; between affirming life, based on the fact that she recognized the values of existence, and denying life, which she had already done, at least in her opinion of herself. Her lifestyle had been utterly inauthentic, and that inauthenticity expressed itself in her world. Her sexual perversion—in which she really did not choose to participate—meant she allowed her husband to choose for her in a region that is her province exclusively. She chose to permit her husband to define her. She bartered her freedom to define herself for his ephemeral promise not to abandon her. That choice was a decision for inauthenticity, a choice for death. But Mrs. Z now realizes that she made that choice against life freely.

The drowning death of her son was a dramatic reflection in the objective world of the selling out of her freedom in the subjective world. When she sold her freedom her world died; the real values of her world were thereby destroyed. When her consciousness sold its freedom, her world died in the form of her precious child. That theme also occurs in John Updike's *Rabbit Run*.

Mrs. Z was in conflict. Her guilt and anxiety were symptoms of her underlying conflict. She chose life to the extent that she was still living and that she voluntarily had herself committed to avoid possible suicide. But she also chose death in that she was responsible for the destruction of her only child. She chose death in that she lived in an intolerable marriage, and in that she lived as an object to be used by her husband, rather than a subject to be encountered by another authentic inwardness. She chose death in the sense that she *let* her life happen rather than *made* it happen.

Her problem was agonizing because she was now in touch with the region of human freedom where choice or decision-making can no longer be postponed, avoided, or repressed. The tragedy of her life forced upon her the truth about human existence.

There is one choice that is not symbolic, but literal; it is a choice that cannot be postponed for even a fraction of a second, because its postponement is already a choice underlying

all other choices. Each person is confronted every living moment with this tremendous dilemma: "Do I choose death? Do I
choose to say yes to life or do I choose to say no to life?" Mrs. Z
had reached, fortunately and unfortunately, the agony of that
ultimate philosophic depth. She was truly in crisis.

For successful existential therapy to take place the therapist
must himself have an authentic philosophic attitude. Mrs. Z's
therapist felt strongly that his patient was not sick, but
healthy; that she was not maladjusted, but confronted with a
philosophical reality. He decided to deal with her problem at
the level of its philosophic depth rather than that of its symp-
tomatic surface. Specifically, the therapist felt that Mrs. Z's
problem was an expression of the authentic structure of existential conflict itself, and that consequently her problem had
no solution and all search for it would thus be futile. Solution
would have meant that the life-death choice had a permanent
and unilateral answer. To recognize that conflict as authentic — even at the unbearable level at which Mrs. Z experienced
it — is the truth about humanity. She can live with it. We all
live with it, and are stronger and more real for living with it.
And she can reconstruct her life on her strengths thus discovered.

Furthermore, Mrs. Z's problem, her therapist recognized,
was but a metaphor — a powerful one, needless to say — for the
field of consciousness. Her problem is a by-product of human
nature itself. Her agonizing dilemma, between life and death,
depression and joy, failure and success, is but a blurred photograph of consciousness. Mrs. Z's problem reflects the incom-
patibility between the subjective and the objective regions of
the field of consciousness that is the universe.

Her problem also reflects the meaning of freedom, which is
always confronted with at least two alternatives from which to
choose. And the existential message is that the truth makes
you strong. If it should happen that the truth makes you
weak — as it did Mrs. Z at the time of her admission to the hospital — it is because of an inability to accept philosophic realities. Had she accepted earlier the ambiguities of human na-

ture and her consequent responsibility, she would not have
been in the mess in which she found herself. But she was able
to accept the present chaos of her life as a further expression of
humanity's ambiguities. Once that was done, she found the
strength to reorganize her life and to assume responsibility for
its betterment.

Mrs. Z was now ready for the lessons of existential philosophy. Thus, her therapist recognized genuine hope and good
news beneath all her despair and anxiety, depression and
guilt. Why? Because she was at that moment in touch with the
freedom of her consciousness and with its bipolarity. *These are
the resources for authenticity in all human beings.* These existential ideas were always kept alive in the mind of the therapist
and gave direction to his strategy in treating Mrs. Z.

It was made clear to Mrs. Z, using many of the techniques of
psychotherapy, that the point she then reached in her therapy—the experiences of freedom and of contradiction—was
really a condition of health and authenticity. She reached a
point where mature philosophic self-knowledge was not only
possible but forced itself on her. She was not sick: She had
reached the center of her authenticity, her health. Her problem was the surface appearance of a universal philosophic
truth. She had to wrestle with that truth not just for herself
but, heroically, for all mankind. The therapist's attitude as
well as his words conveyed this message.

The therapeutic consequences to Mrs. Z were these: that she
must rest on her anguish, dwell on it, "get into it." She must
train herself, with the aid of her therapist, to let herself go
completely into her anguish by relaxing fully and meditating
on her agony. She must get in touch with the full extent of her
anxiety. She was reassured repeatedly that no worse disaster
would occur; she was physically protected in the hospital setting. In fact, she is already—at this moment in her life—confronting "the worst possible disaster"—that is, the emptiness of
her existential freedom and the conflict between life and
death. Mrs. Z can now live confidently in the full exposure of
her feelings of grief. The healthiest of all experiences, the ex-

perience that yields the maximum amount of strength, is the experience of forcing oneself to face the terrifying abyss of freedom, the horrid emptiness of ambiguity. Because once you have forced yourself to face that fully you know that you have faced *successfully* the ultimate threat; the indestructibility of human consciousness will have flashed into awareness.

When she is thus comfortably close to her feelings and safe at the same time, Mrs. Z goes through violent and powerful expressions of emotion. She screams and weeps, she flails her arms and kicks her feet. She rages and she pounds. All of this is encouraged, as it would be in rage-reduction or primal-scream therapy. These feverish outbreaks of emotion show Mrs. Z the feeling content of her philosophic nature—that is, of the freedom of her consciousness. An existential- philosophic truth can be a fantastically emotional experience. She has discovered that to be human is to face this terror and to discover that such a confrontation is both *possible* and strength-giving. (The major obstacle to this kind of existential therapy is the anxiety it produces in the therapist, not what it does to the patient.)

The next stage for Mrs. Z is to begin making her peace with the existential freedom and existential paradox that she has now confronted within herself. She now feels right about the terror, because the second-order pain is gone. She no longer feels anxious about her anxiety or guilty about her "abnormality" or neurosis. And she feels right about the terror because she has seen that it cannot touch the inward consciousness which she is. She feels strong and human; she has rejoined the healthy mainstream of humankind. She is now working for all of us: as she resolves her problem she also resolves it for history. She has become a philosopher.

There exists a state of being in which one can accept the most intolerable in oneself and in others. Mrs. Z has achieved that state. And that state is a more noble condition than suicide, which was her earlier response to that same intuition. Let us examine how this matter worked itself out in Mrs. Z's existential therapy.

Her therapist led her to fierce and determined suicidal thoughts. Her guilt and sense of worthlessness were so intense that the ultimate act of aggression against the body or the person that lived so sinfully was a reasonable release. Self-murder was the logic of the heart. Mrs. Z dwelt on that stage for three full months in her therapy. Could she say *yes* to life in the presence of all that nothingness? Paul Tillich defines God as the power to resist nonbeing. Mrs. Z is face to face with nonbeing—her guilt, her evil, her depravity, as she sees it. Is nonbeing to win and determine her decision for her?

Mrs. Z reached her existential crisis. The therapist had to stay out of it. The final decision was hers and not that of the therapist. And here the therapist must be a philosopher. The therapist is professionally and legally obligated to save the life of his patient, even if that would lead to a vegetable existence for the latter. In a manner of speaking, the philosopher has no such professional or legal obligation—although he may well have chosen to save a life at all costs as his personal ethical commitment. The philosopher can thus witness—and that is all, just witness, not direct—the agony of the free choice of his patient. The philosopher must accept the patient's choice.

Mrs. Z decided, without prompting and without reference to instinct, that *in spite* of the depravity of her empirical ego she would say *yes* to life. At that moment of crisis she became recreated, rechosen and redefined: She reconstituted and reconstructed herself. She became a different person altogether. A new individual was born. If you walk uphill against a rainstorm you feel strong and real as the sharp wind whips your face and the freezing rain numbs it. To say *yes* to life against the death of her only child because of her irresponsible neglect has the same kind of strength-giving significance. It is difficult to depict this extraordinary and refreshing experience. Yet it is this possibility—which is universal in all of us but made conscious only to a priveleged few—that places human beings outside of the order of nature. It truly makes us supernatural.

Mrs. Z must hold onto her experience and her insight—the noble strength won from ignoble adversity. It is right that she affirm the glory of her life in spite of and against all she despises.

Mrs. Z's explorations into her inwardness have now completely transcended any psychological problem. She is no longer a patient in a hospital, a social pariah, but she has joined the ranks of the world's philosophers. Philosophy is the most ancient of the healing arts. It occupies itself with the ills of being human. She is now ready to come to terms with the problem of evil.

At this stage of her existential "treatment" (her "philosophical development" is a better expression), Mrs. Z developed a spiritual, mind- and consciousness-centered worldview sharply different from the materialistic view she had absorbed from our culture. Her new values were connected with the eternal aspects of human consciousness. Her physical and psychological tensions diminished because her involvement with the world became relaxed and even somewhat aloof rather than compulsive and desperate. She now dealt with problems in a global rather than a particularized way. She moved from what had been a mechanical approach to the problems of human existence to a humane approach. Her worldview approached the model of Oriental philosophies—a great peace came over her. It was a peace based on true insights about the nature of man and not on artificial tranquilization. It was an infinite peace based on sharpened and penetrating vision rather than on blocked and dulled sensitivities. She moved away from the object-centered philosophies of the West to the subject-centered philosophies of the East. She experienced a change in attitude, perception, and interpretation. She felt her anguish had been due to blindness and ignorance about the real nature of man and the world in which he exists. She had "converted" from a ghost-in-a-machine theory to a field-of-consciousness theory of humanity. What began as antidepressive therapy concluded with one of the great visions of philosophy.

Involved here is the discovery that this *is* the best of all possible worlds. Only when one identifies one's consciousness with a cosmic consciousness will this be the best of all possible worlds. But this view, for Mrs. Z, can be held only if she does not identify herself exclusively with the fate of a small region of this world: her body, her husband, her boyfriend, or her dead child. Only when her fate is the fate of the universe, only when she thinks of herself as truly a child of the universe will this world — with all the injustices that it visits upon humanity — be to her the best of all possible worlds.

14

The Meaning of Death

Death is the most dramatic reminder of the permanent presence of negation in life. This is a response to a question raised by a nurse attending one of my seminars.

Question: "I am a public health nurse. I work in particular with dying children (leukemia, cancer) and with their parents, but also with dying oldsters in general. How can existential philosophy help me help my patients?"

Answer: Rule number one is for you to achieve authenticity in the area of death yourself. You must understand, first, the full *theoretical* spectrum of the existential philosophy of death and dying and you must learn, second, to fully integrate these intellectual insights into your *experience* and into your life. In other words, to help your patients you yourself must be ready to die today.

But there is more: You must also be able to die with dignity as if you were now a child. Furthermore, you must be capable of managing your life as the parent of a dying and then a dead child; and finally you must be able to die as an old person, even in agony and loneliness. Once you are ready, you can help your patients.

If you have gone through the intellectual work of understanding and then through the emotional work of coming to terms with these issues, the practical question of how to help your patients is relatively minor. Most of what is then needed is for you, as an authentic person, to make yourself available to them. Individuals who seek mere *techniques* for the management of the emotionally stricken may in reality wish to bypass any personal involvement with and personal commitment to the afflicted patient. However, it is precisely this ability to make a commitment to the patient that will help him. When a nurse seeks techniques she is in effect asking to be transformed into a health machine that will "cure" philosophical or existential ills automatically, forgetting that what heals philosophic ills, such as fear of inevitable death, is love, devotion, and commitment. The personal relationship and not the technique has the healing powers. The belief that a purely technological approach to inevitable death is even theoretically possible is evidence of total inauthenticity; it is proof of having completely misunderstood the nature of man, especially the dimension of intimacy, of shared subjectivities.

Rule number two is to understand the philosophical elements in the management of death. These make up the heart of an existential personality theory.

An individual whose life is relatively uneventful will manage death with modest success if he adopts the first solution to what in existential philosophy I call "the paradox of self-transcendence"—the conscious *repression* of philosophical themes. Many people go through life easily without ever seriously contemplating death. You, as a public health nurse, have made the contemplating of death your profession, the center of your life.

What does the knowledge of death do to the healthy individual? Only when that question is answered can we deal with the sick. In your case, the healthy ones are the *parents* of dying children. To them, the philosophical truth about death means the discovery of (1) life's true values and (2) life's true limits.

Confronted with death—any death whatever—that of a pet, a child, a grandparent, a stranger, or your own—an individual immediately recognizes what values are important and which are not. For the nurse speaking to parents, this insight means she should focus no only on the values lost but also on the values remaining, as well as those still to be created. For instance, there may be other children; if not, the parents might have or adopt additional children. The values of being a child and of being a parent remain. In fact, the death of a child immeasurably enhances the values of *all* children and of *all* parents. The death of a child sanctifies the values of childhood and parenthood. True, the love for the new children can never make up for the lost child. But new children are loved more intensely, warmly, and meaningfully with a love that is nurtured on the soil of the dead child. And that places in sharp focus the divine value of a human consciousness.

Furthermore, the death of their child represents limitation for the parents. Death is coming; that is a fact. No one and nothing can change that fact. And that fact is bad; it seems to be the worst that can happen to anyone. It is the fate and nature of man to be condemned by these boundaries, these impenetrable barriers. To be human is to be (unfairly) limited in this way. But to be fully human is also to genuinely want to live with these boundaries: that is the difference between the infinity of God and the finitude of humans.* Wanting to be human is wanting to be limited. And the ability to confront death is the proof of that want.

How can a nurse get these abstract philosophic ideas across to the living needs of the parents of a dying child? She can focus on the reality of the situation. She can emphasize that the child *will* die and call attention to the fact that death is indeed a tragedy and terrible injustice, without redemption. She can help make clear to the parents that they, as human beings, are absolutely limited, that we all are the prisoners of our own humanity. She must avoid all statements that indicate there is hope for the child or that his death is not as tragic as was really thought. The burial of the child is necessary—painful as it is for the family—to make clear to all the absolute finality of death. That finality must be faced and confronted even before the death of the child. Absolute limits and impenetrable barriers define our humanity.

The nurse might help by calling attention to *other* limits in their and others' lives. The parent himself may have lost a par-

---

*We can think of God and man as part of a continuum: the eternal struggle between the finite and the infinite which is the mystery of existence. The infinite chooses to be finite while still retaining the desire for infinity.

ent, or he may even have lost his own childhood in a war or depression. He may have lost the opportunity for education or for the pursuit of a talent. To those who are well, the survivors of the dead, a philosophical analysis of death enhances seriousness about life by eliciting man's true values and realistic limits.

But this approach is for the living, not for the dying, because these comments regarding the confrontation with our limits are principally for the healthy. Death only vitalizes those who can reasonably expect to look forward to some substantial and heady living. Those who are about to die must be treated far more carefully and on separate principles. Death has a different meaning for those who know they are about to die than for those who believe they have much life left in them. In determining what approach to take, the crucial question that the nurse must answer is "What is my patient's concept of death?"

Since no one living has died, for each of us the death of our subjective consciousness is but a speculative belief. It is this belief that makes us human.

An old person must be given serious hope for the indestructibility of consciousness. That can be done through philosophical analysis or religious metaphor. The dying patient who has had time to prepare himself is usually peaceful and even joyous. He experiences the peace of one who knows that he is an indestructible consciousness not necessarily involved with the world. The dying person who is reconciled in this fashion has become in effect the saintly ascetic revered by all the world cultures in all periods of history. He participates in his death.

You would like to be able to tell your dying patients "Death is not the end." As a nurse dealing with the dying, you hope that the notion of immortality—that is, the idea that consciousness is an Eternal Now and that time is outside the consciousness—can be supported philosophically. Can you accept that? Can you accept it theoretically? Practically and feelingly? Your answer, as a nurse, has to be *yes* if you are to be fully effective.

Here is a letter from a friend that, in the context of Alcoholics Anonymous, begs to substitute the philosophical idea of the indestructible consciousness for the religious belief in immortality:

Dear Dr. Koestenbaum:

Just some quick comments about the chapter in your book (*The Vitality of Death*) about "Phenomenology of Religion." As you know, because of my AA training I have come to depend a great deal upon a "Higher Power" to get sober and stay sober in AA. For 10 years this "Higher Power" has been represented by my "AA Group." I have not been able to accept the "God Concept" or the "Spiritual Thing" because of my disastrous 16 years of Catholic schooling.

I am now ready to accept intellectually and emotionally your phenomenological concept of "my pure subjective consciousness" as my "Higher Power." However, I would like your personal comments to me about this — perhaps on the phone later this week, if possible.

The writer suffers, literally, from the "death of God," the malady that was first described by Nietzsche. He hopes the existential notion of pure consciousness can serve as substitute for his lost but needed God. But a concept alone cannot take the place of a living experience and vibrant reality. He needs a friend, one who cares and who loves, one who is permanently and fully available — a person who should have been but was not present in his childhood. He needs evidence of another consciousness connected to his consciousness. It is not enough for him to understand the principles of existential philosophy; he must also experience their meaning in the manner in which he lives. Existential philosophy cannot be understood fully in one's study — any more than one can live fully there. Understanding also means action, and above all, relations with people, commitment to people — interactions of consciousnesses. That is where the nurse can enter in. She is the conscious contact, the intersubjective presence, because she has made a commitment to the patient until he dies!

The child, however, does not really know that he is dying. He does sense the anxiety of his parents and thus fears something dreadful, even worse than death itself. His life must nevertheless continue normally, unchanged, with hope, tenderness, and the full presence and availability of the consciousness of his parents.

When a child has hope he possesses in effect an unadulterated sense of time. To be alive in the world means to have become time. Time is always directed into the future. To experience time as a continuum that is rooted in the present and uses the past in order to point to the future is the authentic time — the future for him must always exist. It is the privileged challenge of the parents and the nurse to create an emotional and educational environment for the child in which he can have a future - and growth-oriented life. The child must continue to enjoy a humanistic education: literature and the arts, philosophy and religion, and above all, the love and intimacy of other human beings.

Shakespeare expressed himself masterfully on the subject of death when he wrote:

Cowards die many times before their deaths,
The valiant never taste of death but once.
Of all the wonders that I yet have heard,
It seems to me most strange that men should fear,
Seeing that death, a necessary end,
Will come when it will come.

Julius Caesar, Act II, scene ii.

These are the basic points to remember in the management of death:

1. To help others with death you must first have come to terms with your own death, both intellectually and emotionally.

2. Specifically, you must have made your peace with four possible kinds of death:

    a. your death now;

    b. your death if you were now a child;

    c. the death of your child or a loved one now;

    d. your death as an old and ailing person.

3. Techniques to help the dying are meaningless, because

death is a philosophical problem rather than a medical one. Consider that there is no cure for death!

4. To help the dying you must understand the existential ideas regarding death.

5. Many people repress the fact of death.

6. Knowledge of death helps us understand the true values of life.

7. Knowledge of death helps us understand the true limits of human existence.

8. It is necessary to point out the increase in the remaining values and obligations because of the death of a loved one.

9. It is necessary to point out the deep meaning of the finitude of humanity made apparent by the death of a single person.

10. The question of the eternity of consciousness should be raised with adults directly and with children indirectly.

11. The dying should be helped as far as possible to retain hope and a sense of time that moves into the future.

Conclusion
The Philosopher

The role of philosophy and of the philosopher has not changed since Socrates. Professional philosophers are rare; that is, there are few of them. They often are lonely, rejected, and frequently they are completely, even deliberately, misunderstood. What the philosopher has to say is not a truth like a chemical equation, which exists safe at a distance from the living human libido, but is an individual statement, a personal commitment wrought out of him or her through the strenuous agony of reality itself.

Philosophers practicing philosophy are more like prophets than they are like professionals. They must be individuals and act as individuals, for they are unprotected by any guild. Their essential and individual being are on the line. They are not guarded by a group—a profession, a school, a legal entity, a religion or a tradition. They cannot hide. They are themselves and they are alone. And in so living they cannot help themselves. They do not want to be martyrs: they do not relish persecution; nor do they desire to be misunderstood. But their commitment to be genuine individuals, true human beings—not carbon copies of what happens to be popular or safe—is but a statement of the universal human essence.

The role of philosophers in America is not unlike the role of the poet and the novelist in Russia. Like Socrates, they are the conscience of all individuals. They are not a conscience in the sense of setting moral rules, not at all. Philosophers are the conscience of people because they remind people of the nature of their humanity. And when people are confronted with the ultimate philosophical realities of their human nature, they run away, deny, attack, ignore or destroy. Why? Because much of what goes under the name of living is really dying. For many, the project of life becomes how to maximize self-deception. For others, life is really ignorance of life. And when confronted with their assumptions, people are threatened and defend themselves with their ignorance. The wages of integrity is injustice.

Why is philosophy threatening? Philosophers think to the roots. That means they first uncover assumptions and then question them. They are honest in their work. They are both logical and empirical, both rational and intuitive, both thoughtful and observant. They are logician and scientist, mathematician and artist. When the questioning of assumptions is integrated into a person's life, then the experience is more like an earthquake or a tornado than a game of chess or a crossword puzzle. When the question becomes "What are my assumptions?" then the desperate defenses of the psychological organism close ranks for a last stand.

Let me now be specific. What is personalized education in philosophy? Education in philosophy is the effort and the desire to help an individual understand himself or herself philosophically. It was to this goal that Nietzsche and Kierkegaard devoted their lives. Education in philosophy is to help an individual see what is going on in his or her life in the area of basic philosophical issues and assumptions. Personalized education in philosophy is to discover, in one's own existence, the meaning of life. Personalized education in philosophy is to experience the power of these questions: "What is the meaning of my life?" "*Does* my life have any meaning?" "*Should* my life have meaning?" "What do I search for, in the quest for meaning?" "Is there any meaning to the question of my meaning?"

I ask "Is it not dangerous, or at least unethical, to pretend that one can help an individual with his or her philosophical agony, with the problem of giving significance, reality, and meaning to his or her life, by using not the science of humanity (which is philosophy) but the science of animals (which is biology and physiology) and the science of sand, stones and water (which is chemistry and pharmacology)?" Fortunately, most individuals in the healing arts are people first and professionals second, guaranteeing in this manner that in truly helping others they are doing philosophy through the language of one of the natural or life sciences. Philosophy is not primarily concerned with mental illness. Personalized education in philosophy begins with a healthy person and helps him or her through the universal human stresses present even in the most successful of people: love, independence, death, suffering, frustration, compassion and responsibility.

The questions that are brought to the philosophical consulting room have to do with the nature and authenticity of consciousness. They are particular and personal questions. It is unethical, irrelevant, and even damaging to handle the problems of consciousness (or *spirit*) without recognizing their deeply philosophic character. These questions cannot be dealt with in terms of childhood experiences or behavior modification. To do so may lead people to believe they are dealing successfully with problems related to the meaning of life, when actually they may never have confronted the true issues underlying their anxiety and pain. Fortunately there are many outstanding human beings in the healing professions who, though they may not be fully conscious of it, perform a philosophic function as they practice their healing arts. But how much more efficacious it is to be fully aware as one searches for a more satisfactory way of life!

Personalized education in philosophy, which we have explored in this book, enables us to come to terms in our own personal lives with such philosophic problems as the relationship between mind and body, thought and feeling. We come to grips with the question of human freedom, not in abstract and universal terms, but in our own lives and experiences. With personalized education in philosophy, each person encounters the issue of the reality of other minds and with it the corresponding question of ethics in human relationships. In personalized education in philosophy the individual comes to know the characteristics of his or her own consciousness—how it constructs meanings or fails to do so.

Personalized education in philosophy also concerns itself with the question of the individual's own personal death and how to manage it. It deals with the relation of the individual to whatever the word *God* stands for in his or her life. It deals furthermore with the meaning of love—one of the most crucial philosophical themes. Finally, personalized education in philosophy concerns itself with the choice of values. We must all live and rear our children by values we believe to be true. This is not an academic question; it is a personal one. It is not a question of the mind, nor is it one of the body. It vibrates through the total human being. It is a question each of us must answer. The philosopher spends a lifetime wrestling—alone—with these questions. And we are all philosophers.

Index

Peter Koestenbaum is Professor of Philosophy at San Jose State University in California. He has received the Trustees' statewide Outstanding Professor Award of the California State University and College system, and he directs the Institute for Clinical Philosophy in San Jose, California.

His other books are:

Existential Sexuality: Choosing to Love. Englewood Cliffs, NJ: Prentice-Hall, 1974
Is There an Answer to Death? Englewood Cliffs, NJ: Prentice-Hall, 1976.
The New Image of the Person. Westport, CT: Greenwood Press, 1978.
The Vitality of Death: Essays in Existential Psychology and Philosophy. Westport, CT: Greenwood Press, 1971.

BOOKS OF RELATED INTEREST

LOVE IS LETTING GO OF FEAR by Gerald G. Jampolsky, M.D., is based on materials from *A Course In Miracles* which teaches us to let go of fear and remember that our very essence is love. To experience the kind of reality we need, we must be willing to bypass our old, logical, rational type of thinking. 128 pages, soft cover, $4.95

THE HEALING MIND, Rev. Ed., by Dr. Irving Oyle effectively presents an alternative to the established medical process. Inner belief is a vital factor in any healing process and whatever you put your faith in can be the precipitating agent for your own return to good health. 160 pages, soft cover, $4.95

MIND THERAPIES, BODY THERAPIES by George J. Feiss makes it possible to distinguish one from the other of the many therapies available and includes explanations of what active involvement in each technique entails. Complete listing of resource materials is provided. 160 pages, soft cover, $5.95

HIDDEN MEANINGS is an insightful book which defines words and phrases of everyday usage, and decodes expressions and tones to reveal the true message. Gerald Walker Smith is a psychologist who practices in the San Francisco area. 160 pages, soft cover, $4.95

In psychologist Bruce Davis' THE MAGICAL CHILD WITHIN YOU a disarmingly simple and direct introduction to the child we each have to raise — the child in our own hearts — is made. Winsomely illustrated by Genny Wright. 112 pages, soft cover, $3.95

Available at your local book or department store or directly from the publisher. To order by mail, send check or money order to:

Celestial Arts
231 Adrian Road
Millbrae, CA 94030

Please include $1.00 for postage and handling. California residents add 6% tax.